youngwriters 2006 Poetry Competition

"I have a dream t
children will one day
where they will not l
color of their skin, l
of their character."

Martin Luther King

I have a dream

words to change the world

- MOTIVATE your pupils to write and appreciate poetry.
- INSPIRE them to share their hopes and dreams for the future.
- BOOST awareness of your school's creative ability.
- WORK alongside the National Curriculum or the high level National Qualification Skills.
- Supports the *Every Child Matters - Make a Positive Contribution* outcome.
- Over £7,000 of great prizes for schools and pupils.

"When I was out there I was never ever
alone, there was always a team of people
behind me, in mind if not in body."

Ellen MacArthur

Reality Bites!
Edited by Allison Dowse

 Young**Writers**

First published in Great Britain in 2006 by:
Young Writers
Remus House
Coltsfoot Drive
Peterborough
PE2 9JX
Telephone: 01733 890066
Website: www.youngwriters.co.uk

SB ISBN 1 84602 646 6

Foreword

Imagine a teenager's brain; a fertile yet fragile expanse teeming with ideas, aspirations, questions and emotions. Imagine a classroom full of racing minds, scratching pens writing an endless stream of ideas and thoughts . . .

. . . Imagine your words in print reaching a wider audience. Imagine that maybe, just maybe, your words can make a difference. Strike a chord. Touch a life. Change the world. Imagine no more . . .

'I Have a Dream' is a series of poetry collections written by 11 to 18-year-olds from schools and colleges across the UK and overseas. Pupils were invited to send us their poems using the theme 'I Have a Dream'. Selected entries range from dreams they've experienced to childhood fantasies of stardom and wealth, through inspirational poems of their dreams for a better future and of people who have influenced and inspired their lives.

The series is a snapshot of who and what inspires, influences and enthuses young adults of today. It shows an insight into their hopes, dreams and aspirations of the future and displays how their dreams are an escape from the pressures of today's modern life. Young Writers are proud to present this anthology, which is truly inspired and sure to be an inspiration to all who read it.

Contents

Allertonshire School, Northallerton

Katie Scott-Marshall (13) 1
Emma Holmes (13) 1
Georgina Ryall (13) 2
Lucy Atkinson (13) 3
Clare Lake (13) 4
Hannah Whyman (13) 5
Jennifer Langthorne (12) 5
Elisabeth Walters (13) 6
Ben Wilson (12) 6
Charlie Teasdale (13) 7
Greg Ient (12) 8
Jack Zelenka (12) 9
Stephen Youll (13) 9
Diane Langthorne (12) 10
Amy Bond (13) 11
Jacob Sankey (13) 12
Lisa Cook (13) 13
Claire Mitchell (13) 14
Beth Matthews (13) 15
Clare Eames (13) 16
Sophie Walker (13) 16
Samuel Greaves (13) 17
Jessica Sadler (13) 17
Emma Harston (12) 18
Thomas Butler (13) 19
Christina Mitchell (13) 20

Biddulph High School, Biddulph

Josh Whitehurst (14) 20
Hannah Whitehurst (16) 21
Jake Murphy (15) 22
Philippa Longmore (14) 23
Jessica Fitzgerald (15) 24
Liam Shropshire-Fanning (14) 24
Jon Turnock (14) 25
Reece Joyce (13) 25
Rach Facey (14) 26
Stuart Siddall (13) 26

Cheryl Ingram (14)   27
Maxine Boulton (14)   27
Helen Lally (13)   28
Lydia Potts (14)   29
Amy Cliffe (15)   30
Holly Elliott (14)   31
Catherine Managh (14)   32
Emma Cocking (15)   33
Amy Gerrard (13)   33
Georgina Wright (15)   34
Sophie Barber (14)   35
Charlotte Copestick (14)   35
Jessica Herrington (15)   36
Jon Carney (14)   36

Branston County Junior School, Branston
Lucy Helas (11)   37
Jamie Wharton (10)   38
Oliver Wake (9)   38
Chloe Souter (11)   39
Jed Willcox (11)   39
Melissa Bush (11)   40
Oliver Bentley (11)   40
Nicholas Huxtable (11)   41
Abi Davis (11)   41
Sam Burnett (11)   42
Bethany Donaldson (11)   42
Sophie Brown (11)   43
Joe Robinson (11)   43
Eden Haytree (11)   44
Ben Samways (11)   44
Jade Lee (11)   45
Gabriella Hill (10)   45
Frances Payne (11)   46
Lucia Brown (11)   47
Amy Townsend (10)   47
Danny Read (11)   47
Tia Wake (11)   48
Wade Garrett (11)   49
Amy Wallis (11)   49
Daniel Davis (11)   50

Castle Rushen High School, Castletown

Heather Booth (12)	50
Lydia Harris (12)	51
Chloe Sullivan (12)	51
Philip Cringle (12)	52
Katie Gilson (12)	52
Terence Lennon (11)	53
Abigail Swayne (12)	53
Zack Skuszka (12)	54
Catreeney Harkin (12)	54
Thomas Richardson Hall (11)	55
Kayleigh Masson (12)	55
Ruby Callister (12)	56
Tom Bowden (12)	56
Kieran Tildesley (12)	57
Harry Harrison (12)	57
Patrick Gandy (11)	58
Ferghal Clucas-Morris (12)	58
Blaine Perston (12)	59
Bethany Quayle (11)	59
Daniel Price (12)	60

De Ferrers Technology College, Burton upon Trent

Kirsty Lane (13)	60
Chloe Bayston (13)	61
Jenny Heathcote (13)	62
Emily Moss (13)	62
Elina Baker & Emily Moss (13)	63
Christopher Moss (13)	64
Nadia Saghir (12)	64
Daniel Jones (12)	65
Mariam Begum (12)	65
Rachel Freeman (11)	66
Daniel Carter (13)	66
Emily Lakin (13)	67
Liam Anguish (12)	67
Louisa Statham (12)	68
Jack Roberts (12)	68
John O'Brien (12)	69
Shane Gregory (12)	69
Joe Wheeler (13)	70

De La Salle College, St Saviour

Harrison Collins (12)	70
Miles Thompson (12)	71
Frederick Kelleher (12)	71
Charles Hubert (12)	72
Alexander Mayes (12)	72
Robin Martins (12)	72
Louis Richardson (12)	73
David Jolley (12)	73
Mitchell Dellar-Crone (12)	73
Chris Bellot (13)	74
George Eddie (12)	74
Aaron Labey (13)	75
Aaron Quinlan (12)	75
Stephen Le Brun (14)	76
Anthony Regan (14)	76
Jason Higgins (14)	77
Alexander Carpenter (14)	77
Ciaran Tyrrell (11)	78
Heller Garcia (12)	78

Elizabeth College, St Peter Port

James Chan (12)	79
James Firth (12)	79
Nathanial Eker (11)	80
Nicholas Harris (13)	81
Nicholas Kerins (12)	82
Ryan Ferbrache (12)	82
Jean-Pierre Payne (12)	83
Henry Carre (13)	84
Alex Wilson (13)	85
Alex Lacey (12)	85
Michael Hart (13)	86
Josh Cutter (13)	86
Elliot R Clark (13)	87

Farnborough School Technology College, Clifton

Katie Prest (14)	87
Holly Brindley & Paula Lydamore (13)	88
Anthony Leeming (15)	89
Zak Thresher (13)	89

James Colagiovanni (14)	90
Deneesh McDonald (14)	91
Michelle Bull & Laura Spencer (14)	92
Emma Clarke (15)	93
Jamie Birch (15)	94
Thomas Wheadon (14)	94
Nikita Adkin (15)	95
Kayleigh Desnos (13)	96
Robert Parnham (14)	97
Erln Bower (14)	98

Hagley Park Sports College, Rugeley

Elizabeth Murray (15)	99
Amber Harrison (15)	100
Robert Murdoch (15)	101

St James' School, Grimsby

Ashley Draper (13)	101
Daisy Jones (13)	102
Alice Twomey (13)	103
Sarah Browne (15)	104
Holly Tumber (13)	104
Rebecca Procter (12)	105
Lucy Smith (13)	106
Anon	106
Amelia Carroll (12)	107
Mia Champion (14)	108
Brian McCarthy (13)	108
Oliver Woods (12)	109
Nicolas Kong (13)	109
Damon Williams (12)	110
Dean Parkinson (12)	110
Charles Sears (12)	111

St Sampson's Secondary School, St Sampson's

Georgia Pengelley (11)	111
David Wickham (12)	112
Daniel Ridley (11)	113
Leanne Oliver (11)	114
Daniel De Carteret (11)	114
Bethany De La Mare (11)	115

Natalie Miranda (12)   115
Will Garnett (12)   116
Marcus Heaume (12)   116
Rachel Tulie (11)   117
Donna Gallienne (12)   117
Adrian Lancaster (12)   118
Elise De La Mare (12)   118

Swanmore Middle School, Ryde
Jennie Wheeler (13)   119
Harry Brown (12)   119
Kara Gregory (13)   120
Dennis Kurtin (11)   120
Louisa Johns (13)   121
Tommy Andrews (13)   122
Jake Mummery (12)   122
Amy Smith (13)   123
Rosie Barrett (13)   124
Michelle Turpin (13)   125
Oliver Ryan (13)   126
Archie Sampson (12)   127
Nico Burns (13)   128
Eloise de Carvalho (12)   129
Grace Hannington (12)   130
Tom Taylor (11)   130
Reegan Greenwood (11)   131
Kym Tims (12)   131
Joe Peduzzi (12)   132
Mollie Valvona (12)   132
Cassandra Loe (12)   133
Emma Beak (12)   134

The Channel School, Folkestone
Laura Stevens (13)   134
Karianne Jewkes (12)   135
Danielle Gough (14)   135
Stephanie Cole (12)   136
Nicola McDonagh (14)   136
Christopher Hadlington (13)   137
Megan Hart (14)   137
Francisco Gomes (14)   138

Sabrijan Juniku (14)	138
Mikyla Melville (12)	139
Rachael Whittle (13)	140
Michael Hunt (12)	140
Cade Mortimer (13)	141
Cameron Jackson (12)	141
Sian Beer (13)	142
Paul Williams (14)	142
Ross Williams (13)	143
Dominic Deeley (12)	144
Liam Staveley (12)	144
Elliot Ranford (12)	144
Hayley Langton	145
Jess Bunker	145
Alex Smith (13)	145
Scott Wilson (12)	146
Daniel Cole (12)	146

Thomas Alleynes High School, Uttoxeter

Rosie Smith (14)	146
Alison Averill (14)	147
Stacey Bettney (15)	148
Daniel Ardron (15)	148
Georgie Nash (15)	149
Sharnie Podmore (13)	150
Daniel Guymer (14)	150
Clarissa Johnson (14)	151
Tiffany Leadbetter (14)	152
Amy Lowe (14)	153
Paige Martin (14)	154
Jonathan Nash (13)	154
Anna Holdcroft (14)	155
Kirsty Pearson (14)	155
Holly Dunn (14)	156
Elizabeth Smith (15)	157
James Teasdale (14)	158
Pete Hoptroff (14)	159
Phil Browning (13)	160
Matt James (14)	161
Katy O'Brien (14)	162
Elliot Allison (14)	162

Paul Slaney (13) 163
Jacques Coetzee (14) 163
Sarah Flavell (14) 164
Jake Thomas (14) 165
Matthew McNeice (13) 166
Demi Wibberley (14) 167
Alice Lewis (14) 168
Lucas Shaw (15) 169
Charlotte Machin (14) 170
Andrew Smy (14) 171

The Poems

In An Alternative Reality A Young Girl Is Dreaming

My nightmare
A world where discrimination is dominant
And justice and happiness are unimportant
A world where poverty, death, abuse and destruction
Overwhelms so many and they cannot function
I break out in sweat as I see the faces
Of people engulfed in anger and hatred
My nightmare briefly breaks off and I open my eyes
To allow myself to sink in all I despise
Clenching my fists and gritting my teeth
I dream of a way to overcome the grief
A world where sexism and racism will vanish
A world where all of its demons are banished
A world where all dreamers are inspired
By ridding the world of all its liars
How mankind can change for the better
And war will stop on the battlefield
I relax as the sun begins to beam
This is my fantasy world. This is my dream.

Katie Scott-Marshall (13)
Allertonshire School, Northallerton

It Doesn't Matter What Race You Are

It doesn't matter what race you are
Or even if you don't like each other
So go talk to that boy over there
And treat him like your brother
Although you may look different
On the inside you're not a world apart
Look through the colour of his skin
And see deep within
Because his heart is pure like yours
If only you could see past the colour
He really could be your brother.

Emma Holmes (13)
Allertonshire School, Northallerton

Through A Child's Eyes

A child's mind is perfection they often ignore,
Those giants who tower, they must be more
Of an angel than us,
But how can they know when they're clouded with hurt?
The child or the adult, who should die first?

For every curl; a child has cried,
For every eyelash; a murder goes unjustified.
For every freckle; a young girl's fate,
For every dimple; once again it's too late.

But a child, one child, any child.

A vision of pure sweet innocence,
Glee and joyous indifference
Seeing what is wrong and right
Minds unpoisoned by greed and spite
Being unafraid of tears
That wash away our darkest fears
Eyes of youth warm the cold outside
Ignite the loving flame inside.

They smile in the face of danger
And chuckle in the face of lies
And won't ignore the hungry stranger
As his faith in mankind dies.

My dream is that we see through a child's eyes
That we feel the pain and hear the cries
But not just turn and look away
Stop. Help them up, then back to play.

Georgina Ryall (13)
Allertonshire School, Northallerton

Suffocating Under Words Of Sorrow

While people are suffocating under these words of sorrow
Wondering if they will see the daylight of tomorrow
People dying, arguing, fighting over this precious Earth
Wondering if all of this is even worth it
Do you want the children of tomorrow
Suffocating under our words of sorrow?
If you don't, why don't you just think of ways
To guide our future through their precious days
Why don't you go and see for yourself
What lots of pride, but no possessions, these people have got.
Ask yourself, what they have done to deserve this?
Imagine children alone at night, with no one to kiss
A life of simpleness, unhappiness and grief
Not much of any food, especially Sunday beef
Just think how fortunate and lucky you really are
A family, a house and probably a car.
You think it's the end of the world when you don't get
The things you want, finding yourself in debt.
At least you had the money, but it's gone to waste.
People living in the Third World don't even have toothpaste
So do you really need these things
iPods, TVs and diamond rings?
Before you buy, just give a though
Of all the things Third Worlds haven't bought
While some people are suffocating under these words of sorrow
Wondering if they will see the daylight of tomorrow
Why don't you do something today
Instead of being in dismay?

Lucy Atkinson (13)
Allertonshire School, Northallerton

Stand Up

So here I stand, alone, deserted, forsaken
The dark penetrating eyes bearing down on me
Yet no ears turn my way, to hear my plead for freedom
Just the angry eyes and the sharp harsh words of the mouth
Will no one hear the voices crying out to be heard?
The voices uttering their dreams of true life
The voices with their notion of how flesh might *just* be flesh
Skin might *just* be skin
But the mind, and the soul and feelings
Might be much more than the words themselves
How freedom does not need these walls
How peace should not need these wars
And how life would be better without these chains
The voices that claim: This Earth should be a world not a cage
But these words reach no reply, no response
Belief is shot down, destroyed, assassinated
Discord and disagreement means no lone voice may ever speak
Freedom has no meaning, liberty is a hoax
And that knowledge is buried with the truth
And the few who once dared to speak up against lies and deception
Against class discrimination, against racism
Against slavery, against crime
Against
So here I stand alone, deserted, forsaken
But honest, fair and true
Choose where you stand.

Clare Lake (13)
Allertonshire School, Northallerton

I Have A Dream

I have a dream that one day people everywhere
Will come together and join hands
As brother and sister, as old friends and new friends
From enemies to neighbours, from hatred to love
From evil to forgiveness, I have a dream.

I have a dream that one day people everywhere
Will stop fighting and shake hands
As father and son, as mother and daughter,
From war to peace, from arguments to agreement
From selfishness to hope, I have a dream.

I have a dream that one day people everywhere
Will forget their differences and live freely together
As children and adults, as husband and wife,
From crying to laughing, from hindering to helping
From killing to caring
I have a dream that this will become a reality.

Hannah Whyman (13)
Allertonshire School, Northallerton

Dare To Dream

A dream is such a special thing
So private, yet so pure
Some may make you feel ashamed and often quite unsure
But I've dared to dream.
We all have the right
To want to rid the world of all its spite
But the help of one or two is not enough
I want the whole world to help burn the burden of poverty
To overcome the presence of ominous dictators
Do not play the role of the innocent spectator
Don't let the world pass you by without a second thought
You only have one life to live
So don't just act upon a whim
Dare to dream!

Jennifer Langthorne (12)
Allertonshire School, Northallerton

Perfect World

A perfect world would be nice and kind
Everyone with a peaceful mind
There would be no terrorism or war
And all the poor would have more
There'd be no more crime
In a matter of time.
Animals safe, big or small
Trees will grow extra tall
Global warming will forever stop
If we recycle stuff like pots
Racism will cease
And we will live in peace.
There will be no more sorrow
As we look forward to a new tomorrow
A perfect world would be nice and kind
Everyone with a peaceful mind.

Elisabeth Walters (13)
Allertonshire School, Northallerton

My World Dream

Just imagine what the world would be like without poverty and crime
It will never stop no matter how much time
Just imagine what the world would be like without disease and death
People would be so happy they would be struggling for breath
Just imagine what the world would be like without murder and rape
It really would be great if those people could escape
My world dream, my world dream.

Just imagine what the world would be like without drought and war
Let's all try and get right to the core
Just imagine what the world would be like without racism and famine
Why did our world come to this? Why is our world now so grim?
My world dream, my world dream.

Ben Wilson (12)
Allertonshire School, Northallerton

Believe

Here I find myself amongst the dusty grassland
Many brave and loyal soldiers surrounding me
The war goes on, black versus white.

I close my eyes, the many noises I hear
The bombs, the gunshots, people's desperate cries
I count to ten and open my eyes once more.

I breathe in deep, the smells of death fill the air,
A bomb drops down, the smoke in my face
It attacks my throat viciously.

I look around, a white man turns to me
Holds his gun up high and shoots.

I feel a sudden pain in my stomach
As I fall to the floor
The bullet has wounded me badly
I see a pool of my own blood form on the floor.

My eyes slowly close and I block the noise out,
I lay on the floor, not daring to move.

I wake up in a small tent, nurses around me,
I hear them whispering, as they walk away.

My last few moments soon arrived,
I watched as they unplugged my last chance of life,
My heart ached as it shed acid tears, my mind weakening.

The air around me turned viciously cold,
I couldn't think, I couldn't hear, I couldn't smell.

I wish for no one else to die this way
I am black, they are white, so we must fight,
I wish we wouldn't, I wish we couldn't

Nobody deserves to be treated this way
So as I rise to a better place, my words to you,
Are forget about race.

Charlie Teasdale (13)
Allertonshire School, Northallerton

I Have A Dream

I dream that . . .
The world will be free
Free of war and deceit
Free of envy and jealousy

I dream that . . .
The world will be free
Free of money and debt
Free of sadness and depression

I dream that . . .
The world will be free
Free of drugs and fags
Free of drink and wine

I dream that . . .
The world will be free
Free of tramps and beggars
Free of vagabonds and vagrants

I dream that . . .
The world will be free
Free of war and attacks
Free of invasion and siege

I dream that . . .
The world will be free
Free of misery and sorrow
Free of regret and grief

I dream that . . .
The world will be free.

Greg lent (12)
Allertonshire School, Northallerton

I Believe

I believe . . .
In a world without war
No famine and no poverty
No hierarchy
No lower or higher class.

I believe . . .
In a world where the people unite as one
A world not split by race or culture
Black and white, hand in hand.

I believe . . .
In a world full of peace
With no hatred
Just peace.

Jack Zelenka (12)
Allertonshire School, Northallerton

I Have A Dream

A dream of a world
Where no one fears
Peace everywhere
Without any tears.

Where bombs are unheard of
Crime nowhere to be seen
Terrorists forgotten
No evil machine.

Black and white
Together as one
Murder and torture
Hate is all gone.

Stephen Youll (13)
Allertonshire School, Northallerton

Mirrored World

Spinning in your world of coldness
Enveloped by mystic fear
Petrified the darkness stole you
That hides behind your crystal tears
But step out into the brightness
So you can see my dream of a mirrored world.
I want to hold this dream up high and let its sails unfurl
Let it send food to all the hungry
Send help to all that need
Send warmth to let us sleep at night
When nightmares ambush our dreams
So let your dream plant a seed
Where we thought goodness would not grow
And explore new ideas where no one else would go
So let your dreams right the wrongs
And the cruelty that should not be
Make our world free of pollution
And fill it with new-found hope
So people whose lives are too hard find new strength to cope.
Let it crumble all that demeans
And when they say who did this
Reply, the strength of the nation's dreams.

Diane Langthorne (12)
Allertonshire School, Northallerton

I Have A Dream

I have a dream where all grass is green
And it's peaceful everywhere
I have a dream where there are no wars
And no guns to be seen.

I have a dream where all creatures are free
And roam just like they should
I have a dream where all men are kind
And there's no hunting or killing to see.

I have a dream where cruelty is vanished
And humans care for the world
I have a dream for no disasters
And no deaths of innocent people.

I have a dream of calm and peace
A dream of happiness and smiles
I have a dream of no suffering
No illness or disease.

If everyone worked as a team
Then all of these thoughts would no longer be just a dream.

Amy Bond (13)
Allertonshire School, Northallerton

The Day That Changed The World . . .

When war is over
And poverty is no more,
When crime ceases to exist
The day the world changes . . .

Peace and harmony set in place
No deliberate death
Black and white people hand in hand
The day the world changes . . .

Disease and plague gone forever
In its place is hope
Terrorism wiped out
The day the world changes . . .

Murder and assault will not exist
Under the new rule
Instead people live fulfilled lives
The day the world changes . . .

But will this ever happen
To a world with so much pain?
A world in which it seems this suffering will never end
The day the world changes . . .

And so we must strive hard
To achieve our ultimate goal
A goal which will get closer day by day
The day the world changes . . .

Jacob Sankey (13)
Allertonshire School, Northallerton

In A Perfect World . . .

In a perfect world . . .
There would be no war and violence
No famine nor poverty and hunger nor hate
No terrorism and crime
It is now time.

In a perfect world . . .
Global warming would stop forever
Disease would be cured
Natural disasters would come to an end
The broken ozone would mend.

In a perfect world . . .
Animals wouldn't be extinct
They wouldn't be neglected or abused
They wouldn't be abandoned and sore
Animal abuse would be no more.

In a perfect world . . .
There would be no child abuse
Animals would not be hunted for trophies and sport
Trees would still grow high in the sky
And on our Earth litter and pollution would not lie.

But we don't live in a perfect world.

Lisa Cook (13)
Allertonshire School, Northallerton

Imagine

Imagine that no one is dying,
Imagine that no one is crying.

Imagine that there are no wars
Imagine that no one breaks the laws.

Imagine that there is no crime,
Imagine that people feel safe all the time.

Imagine that everyone's sons and daughters
Always have clean water.

Imagine that there is no more pollution
That we've discovered an eco-friendly solution.

Imagine that there is no terrorism
And that there are less people in the prisons.

Imagine that there are no animals in danger
And that we are able to talk to strangers.

Imagine that this is our world
It might take years, even centuries
To improve it for the better.

But why not start today?
If we all change things in a little way
This *could* be our world some day!

Claire Mitchell (13)
Allertonshire School, Northallerton

Poverty

Have you ever known
What it's like to be alone?
Cherishing each precious hour of your life
Wondering what the next day will bring
More hunger, more war, more neglect and suffering?

Hoping for something positive
To overcome the troubles
Of the life you live.

Living on the street
Mud and waste beneath your feet.

Do you take your life for granted?
Is it always want, want, want?
That word so often chanted.

Look around to all the people you see
How many of them are happy and free?

Do you really need all these man-made luxuries?
Like PlayStations, computers and TVs?
It's not a case of what we want, but a case of what we need
Don't give the children of the Third World countries
So many reasons to plead
Try and give to charity to help them to succeed
It's not a case of what we want; it's a case of what we need.

Beth Matthews (13)
Allertonshire School, Northallerton

They Have A Voice Inside Them

I have a voice inside me,
A voice that always grows,
They have a voice inside them,
But no one even knows.

If someone pays attention
To the people far away
We can help them to survive
For another day.

When there is no poverty,
They can really smile
And when there is no hunger,
Their lives will be worthwhile.

I have a voice inside me,
A voice that will always grow
They have a voice inside them,
Which everyone should know.

Clare Eames (13)
Allertonshire School, Northallerton

Imagine

Imagine a world where there's peace,
Where we get what we need,
But have no enemies.

Imagine a world where we speak our minds,
Where we're not afraid to say what we think.

Imagine a world where there is no war,
Where we have clean water and a place to live.

I write a song with the future of the world in my heart
So imagine the world as if it's your own
And think what you would do to change it.

Imagine . . .

Sophie Walker (13)
Allertonshire School, Northallerton

Dream

Dream, a world at peace,
Like Spain, France and Greece.
Dream, a world of friends,
Where hatred ends.
Dream, a world of laughing,
People never needing.

Dream, a world, no war,
With no blood or gore.
Dream, a world, no hate,
Where everyone's your mate.
Dream, a world, no fear,
Where no one sheds a tear.

Dream, a world of ours
With many more real powers.
Dream, a world of love,
Carried on the wings of doves.
Dream, dream, dream of
A world . . .

Samuel Greaves (13)
Allertonshire School, Northallerton

I Have A Dream

I have a dream
I fly in the sky.
I have a dream
The world is my parachute.
I have a dream
No poverty, the world is safe.
I have a dream
No war, no fighting.
I have a dream
People singing happily.
I have a dream
Peace . . .

Jessica Sadler (13)
Allertonshire School, Northallerton

A Picture Of A Perfect World

There is a picture on the wall,
A picture of a perfect world.
A picture without any poverty or terrorism,
A picture of a perfect world.

There is a picture on the wall,
A picture of a perfect world.
A picture without racism, where black and white walk hand in hand,
A picture of a perfect world.

There is a picture on the wall,
A picture of a perfect world.
A picture where crime is gone,
Where everyone walks knowing that they are free,
A picture of a perfect world.

There is a picture on the wall,
A picture of no more pain, where no one needs a label to show who
they really are,
A picture of a perfect world.

There is a picture on the wall,
A picture of a perfect world.
A picture where all of these things exist and happiness and love rule,
This is what a perfect world should be.

Emma Harston (12)
Allertonshire School, Northallerton

I Had A Dream . . .

I had a dream that the world was in peace
No war, no envy, no jealousy
If the world had no war and deceit
The world would be the place for me.

I had a dream that litter didn't cover the world
No rubbish, no sewage, no chuddy
If the world had no litter
The world would be the place for me.

I had a dream that wildlife was free
No poachers, no slaughterers, no animal murderers
If the world was free from bad men
The world would be the place for me.

I had a dream that drugs were gone
No cocaine, no speed, no ecstasy
If the world was free from drugs
The world would be the place for me.

To be rid of these burdens of such terror and strain
Without these things the world would be the place for me.

Thomas Butler (13)
Allertonshire School, Northallerton

My Dream

My dream . . .
Walking down the street, seeing people from different cultures shaking
hands.

My dream . . .
Watching other people recycle their rubbish and reusing materials.

My dream . . .
Being able to breathe in clean air and smell the countryside around
me.

My dream . . .
To see the world compromising, forgetting their differences.

My dream . . .
To see the world being fed, homed and clothed.

My dream . . .
To help prevent crime and abuse and help each other.

My dream . . .
For the world to be one happy family and give the world some time.

My dream can be your dream too.

Christina Mitchell (13)
Allertonshire School, Northallerton

I Have A Dream Poem

D oes this mean it will never happen? I asked as I
R ecalled my dream
E ternal peace throughout the world
A cure for illnesses and diseases
M any things could happen to make the world a better place
I magination is a peaceful thing
N ever say never
G o and do something about it. Some day it might come true.

Josh Whitehurst (14)
Biddulph High School, Biddulph

I Have A Dream, Never To Come True

I keep my dreams in a box so they don't get lost,
But still they don't come true.
I waste my time with hope, I am hanging on a rope,
A feeling that isn't new.

I would like a world that's kind, where people speak their mind
And have nothing to fear.
I wouldn't mind a golden age, without anger or rage,
But it won't happen here.

I don't ask for understanding, I am not demanding.
What could that do for me?
I may play a small part, but I have a strong heart
And all I want is to be free.

Some dreams I had as a child were too weird or too wild,
But I remember them well.
If I could help them be real how good I would feel,
Everyone would be able to tell.

What I want most of all is a chance, big or small,
To change and make it snappy.
From the places I've been and the things I have seen
I've thought that I should be happy.

I keep my dreams in a box and although they're not lost
They still have not come true.
I don't think they ever will. Despite this I'm still
Satisfied, how about you?

Hannah Whitehurst (16)
Biddulph High School, Biddulph

I Wish I Were A Bubble . . .

I wish I were a bubble floating way up high
Slowly blown up above into the clear blue sky
I'd love to be a bubble just so that I could show
Just how high I could progress in the world
Just how high that I could go

I wish I were a bubble ascending into space
So I could see the happiness on every passer's face
I'd love to be a bubble just so that I could see
How people live their lives
In total contrast to you and me

I wish I were a bubble so sometimes I could be alone
So that when I wanted no one there
I could just be on my own
Yet I'd love to be a bubble so when I wanted to be
I could be around whoever I wanted
And have them all around me

If I could be a bubble I would be one for a while
So that when I were around I could make some people smile
I would be a little bubble just so that I could be
A little piece of fun and joy
In people that see me

I wish I were a bubble so that when it's time to go
I could say goodbye to everyone, everybody down below
I'd love to be a bubble so that when I say goodbye
I would just pop and that would be the end
Without the pain to die

So if I were a bubble who popped and went away
I'd leave nobody grieving in any sort of way
I'd love to be a bubble as easy it would be
To blow another bubble and 'hello'
Back I would be.

Jake Murphy (15)
Biddulph High School, Biddulph

Dreamer

I lay in my bed one night,
Wondering why I could not sight,
The one true person who I could trust,
The one true person who I must.

That night that person came to me,
In a dream I could see,
The people who inspire me most,
My friends and family and more I boast.

World peace I think would be the best,
Along with friendship which would test,
The new-found love with our friends,
We could make our amends.

My role models I have found,
Are all the people from around,
The ones who work extra time,
To help others to stop crime.

In my dream I also found,
That equality and pollution would be sound,
Remove all of the poverty
And replace it with life quality.

So now I know exactly how,
My new-found trust is needed now,
And that I really have found out,
That we cannot afford to doubt.

Philippa Longmore (14)
Biddulph High School, Biddulph

Dream

This is a poem of my dream land,
A place enriched with sun and sand.
Where fresh wintry water spills from each spring
And an everlasting existence of free birds sing.

I dream of a land where rivers flow,
Where flowers bud and green grass grows.
Clouds roll and play across the sky,
Towering mountains reach up high.

Every person loves with desire
And hope and faith blaze like fire.
Each corner of land is blessed with light
And every eye is shining bright.

All human souls content and pure,
Pain and abuse we no longer endure.
Where a shimmering mist gathers at dawn
A new dream and wish every moment is born.

This is a poem of my dream land,
To make it reality, lend a hand.
Not only a dream should this land be,
But a truth and certainty for all to see.

Jessica Fitzgerald (15)
Biddulph High School, Biddulph

My Dream Poem - Peace

I once had a dream where the Earth was at peace
And the wars of the world were all gone.
The calm of the Earth could be felt out in space
And the thoughts of the world were at one.
What is this force that brings this joy and all of life's desire?
The good of light contained in a void of the wondrous mystical fire
The trees and the birds are all intertwined and mixed in
                                        the ultimate plan
Two become one as they join both halves like a fiery, magical
                                        yin yang.

Liam Shropshire-Fanning (14)
Biddulph High School, Biddulph

I Have A Dream . . .

I have a dream that a voice will say
And guide me to whatever way,
My destiny means to lead me,
Down my chosen pathway, life's key.

And should I fall, come what may,
On the problems plaguing my way,
A gentle hand will pick me up
And push me back into the fray.

Although my legs are aching
And my throat is rough as sand,
My heart is pumping, head thumping,
That voice will pull me over the windswept land.

As I toil across the aged scarred land,
I know I've reached the end, the finish,
Those hands will pick me up
And my weariness will diminish.

I look across the way I've come,
Where others have failed to cross
And that hand, that voice, that warming spirit,
Helps me forget that feeling of loss.

Although I've been drained and sapped of strength
And I don't know where to go,
His tales of laughter show me the way,
With him things will always be just so.

Jon Turnock (14)
Biddulph High School, Biddulph

My Dream Poem

I wish that the things that make us sad or upset were gone
All the people that cause these pains, I wish they were all undone.
They never stop to think about what their actions will cause
Bombers, war and criminals, they deserve no applause.
You don't know what I would pay for these things to go away . . .

Reece Joyce (13)
Biddulph High School, Biddulph

I Have A Dream . . .

I have a dream that we will all come together
So everyone is happy forever and ever . . .
No one is hurt, no one is heartbroken
And everyone is hugely outspoken.
We always speak what's on our mind,
And leave all the bitchiness behind.
The lads finally treat girls right
And no one will ever need to fight . . .
Everyone gets along
And nothing ever goes wrong.
All the evil will back down without a care
So the Twin Towers will still be there.
So work together, it won't even cost a pound,
So the world will be better and everything's sound!

Rach Facey (14)
Biddulph High School, Biddulph

I Had A Dream

I had a dream that I could fly
Took off from the floor and soared through the sky.
In my dream the fields were green
No one was sad and no one was mean.
In my dream the sky was blue
The red sea was red, we all know that's true.
In my dream, race didn't matter
Black people and white came together to chatter.
One day in my life this world green and blue
Hopefully somehow my dream will come true.
So now it's time to say goodbye
Because my dream is going to die.

Stuart Siddall (13)
Biddulph High School, Biddulph

My Dream!

I have a dream . . .
That we all work as a team
So a solution can be found
To keep the world going round.

If we could stop war
Then the world would be pure
We need to start trying
To stop people dying.

If we were all safe
Then the world would be a happier place
Our days would be ace
And we'd save the human race.

I have a dream . . .
That we all work as a team
So a solution can be found
To keep the world going round.

Cheryl Ingram (14)
Biddulph High School, Biddulph

I Have A Dream!

I have a dream that one day everyone will live in peace and harmony.
That there will be no war or fighting
And that everyone will be friends instead of enemies.
I have a dream that everyone will believe in life
That no one will look on the bad side of things
But people will look on the good side of things
That people will always be happy not sad.
I have a dream that everyone will be friends with everyone else
That everyone never argues or fights
And that there is no such thing as bullying
I have a dream!

Maxine Boulton (14)
Biddulph High School, Biddulph

I Have A Dream . . .

I have a dream,
About a big wooden door,
There is a person behind it,
Who can help stop war.

This person can stop poverty,
This person can stop a fight,
This person can be the greatest,
If they try with all their might.

Suddenly something clicks
And the wind begins to whirl,
The door begins to open
And stood behind, there was a girl.

The girl steps forward
And I step back,
But I only do this,
Being scared she might attack.

Quietly she starts to speak
And an idea is meant to be,
But then I realise,
The girl behind the door is me.

Then I started thinking,
That everyone is unique
Anyone can do anything,
If they try to reach their peak.

Helen Lally (13)
Biddulph High School, Biddulph

I Have A Dream!

I have a dream,
I dream of:
Music and laughter,
Love and family,
Fun and games,
Happy ever after.

I dream of:
Ice creams and treats
Biscuits and cakes,
Fresh fruit and marshmallows,
Chocolate and sweets.

I dream of:
Loud noise and tears,
Hate and loneliness,
Work and boredom,
No end to the fears.

I dream of:
Misery and hunger,
Thirst and famine,
Stale bread and sour milk,
Death to the younger.

I have a dream,
But when does my dream become a nightmare?

Lydia Potts (14)
Biddulph High School, Biddulph

No Inspiration

I wish that I could write a poem, that wasn't really bad,
One to laugh, one to cry and one that's really sad.
I obviously can't express my emotions onto a piece of paper,
Well, maybe I could, maybe I can or maybe I'll do it later!

I can't believe that it's so hard to write about a dream
Maybe I need to take a nap and think about what I've seen,
I'm sure I've dreamt of a faraway land
With surfers, waves and golden sand.

But now I can't think of the right words to say,
About my dream from the other day,
Even though it was such a beautiful place,
The words have vanished without a trace.

I'm sure that I am suffering from a poet's curse
Unable to rhyme a simple verse,
Although I'd like to carry on writing
I realise that it's unexciting.

Perhaps next time it might be as well
To dream of a wizard with his magic spell
Who could conjure up the words I need
Without much effort and with lots of speed.

Amy Cliffe (15)
Biddulph High School, Biddulph

I Had A Dream

Last night as I was in my bed
I felt a tap upon my head
I saw a rabbit glowing all white
He looked colourful under the light

He beckoned me to follow him
Out to the night where the moon was dim
We flew across the sleepy city
We told jokes that were witty.

Then we rested on a hill
And imagined a world without kill
We thought of rainbows, flowers and the sun
And realised what now had to be done

No more guns, bombs or war
And let's all find what we're striving for
But soon it was time for home
We took a detour right through Rome

But then I got to my comfy bed
And rested again down my head
I dreamt of a world with so much peace
And in my head, the world was at ease

Holly Elliott (14)
Biddulph High School, Biddulph

I Had A Dream!

I had a dream,
In my dream there was no war,
In my dream nothing was a bore,
In my dream there was no hate,
In my dream everything was fate.

My dream felt real
As if I were awake,
There was fresh green grass
And sparkling blue lakes,
The sky was blue
And the grass was green
I began to believe
It was not a dream.

As I dreamt on no people were selfish,
As I dreamt on no people were thoughtless,
People did love
And people did help
No one was sad
That's what I had felt.

As I awoke my dream faded away
I hoped that my dream would return some day
Back to reality I had started to accept,
As I forgot the dream that I had dreamt.

Catherine Managh (14)
Biddulph High School, Biddulph

Dreams . . .

Every night I fall asleep,
And dream of all the famous people that I could meet.
I scurry from monsters and hide from creatures
And even fear imaginative teachers.

Everyone knows that this fantasy will never reach you,
But I know that one special dream is waiting to come true.
It is seeking for the moment to grab me by surprise,
To make me prosperous and help me rise.

My life will change and reach for the best
But only after passing one final test.
Pleasures in life don't grow on a tree
So I have to work hard if I want them to reach me.

I must jump the hurdles of life,
In order to go forward and strive,
To meet my goals and conquer my fears
Otherwise my dreams could end up in tears.

Emma Cocking (15)
Biddulph High School, Biddulph

I Have A Dream

I have a dream that
Wars, fighting and poverty too
Global warming and terrorism just to name a few
Could all be stopped and we live in peace
Then there is a chance that death could cease.

I have a dream that
Friendship, kindness and love too
Laughter and happiness just to name a few
Could all be shared throughout the Earth
Then this would show mankind's true worth.

Amy Gerrard (13)
Biddulph High School, Biddulph

I Have A Dream

Sometimes I wish that I have wings so I can fly away
Or magic dust to make me disappear
When things get difficult.

Sometimes I wish that I can be somebody else
Just to be free from the hurt and anger
I feel deep within.

Sometimes I wish that I am a genius
Just so that I can succeed in life
As I feel that is the only way to succeed.

Sometimes I wish that I am a confident person
So I wouldn't feel the need to hide the real me.

Sometimes I wish that I am not here
Wishing that I am in another place
Just so I can see how people would react if I was no longer around.

Sometimes I wish that I can be someone rich and famous
Just to make those people who have bullied me
And turned me down wish they hadn't.

Sometimes I wish that I can be free
Just to feel the danger
And sometimes I wish that everything will always go my way
That way I can have everything that I have always wanted.

But at the end of the day, when we hit reality
All I really want is to be happy
And at the moment, I don't feel that way.

My dream is to be happy
From now, until forever.
That is my dream
To be happy.

Georgina Wright (15)
Biddulph High School, Biddulph

I Have A Dream

I have a dream that one day we will all live in peace
And the world will be able to get on as one
And war will just be a nightmare.

I have a dream that Third World countries can get rid of their debt
And starvation and problems and live their lives full
Just as we live ours.

I have a dream that celebrities use their wealth to help others
Who are not as wealthy as they are
And would die for their lifestyle.

I have a dream, the dream to do whatever I want
The freedom I am ever so grateful for, that others cannot have.

My dreams may only be a dream, but to those who live like this
It is their biggest dream and hope.

I have a dream that my dreams will come true one day
And help others just as my life and dreams have helped me.

Sophie Barber (14)
Biddulph High School, Biddulph

I Have A Dream . . .

I have a dream that the world knows no bad.
Heaven is the dream, that all the good have
To feel free and not ruled, that there is no sad.
That we live in a place where everything is our own
And we all have a place that we can call home
Nothing causes pain, suffering or death
All that is left is a place of no stress.
Smiles are the food and frowns are banned
Evil will not be allowed to enter the land.
So this is my dream, I hope it will soon be true
I believe it can be if we unite, the world, me and you.

Charlotte Copestick (14)
Biddulph High School, Biddulph

Dream

I dream of a world without discrimination
A world with all untied nations
Where cruelty and neglect are never known
And no child or person is left alone.
A world full of happiness, love and joy
No one's left out, not girl or boy.
Poverty and disease do not exist
And all temptation we do resist.
Exploding bombs and terror attacks
Are something that this world will always lack.
Endangered species and global warming
A nightmare we leave when we awake in the morning.
My world is simple, my world is just,
But it's only a dream which over I lust.

Jessica Herrington (15)
Biddulph High School, Biddulph

I Have A Dream

The dream that war on Earth will end
Is common and well looked for
And so is the dream that disease will cease
Is looked for often as well.

Many dreams don't happen
Only some dreams come true
People always search for dreams
But only rarely do dreams find you.

But not all dreams are fruitless
All you have to do is try hard
And your dream, it may come true
But wishing won't help you.

Jon Carney (14)
Biddulph High School, Biddulph

I Have A Dream

I once had a dream
I still have that dream
And I am sure
Even in fifty years
I will have that very dream.
I wish people would live in harmony
With mankind and all
To learn to work together
And maybe
It will be that way forever
It has always been about a team
Perhaps people don't realise it
But thanks to our friends and family
Without them we would be nowhere
I once had a dream
I still have that dream
And I am sure
Even in fifty years
I will still have that very dream.
I wish people would never betray
Never break the link
And so what if people stink?
The world is ours so please
I beg you look after it
Who cares what people think of you
It's only you that matters
So please, I am not a cruel or self-hearted person
Remember I have . . . a dream.

Lucy Helas (11)
Branston County Junior School, Branston

I Have A Dream

I have a dream of a perfect world

H earing people scream would not happen
A life that everyone would enjoy
V ery rarely would anything go wrong
E ven on dark and wet days there would be a warm feeling
    inside everyone

A world of happiness

D reams would become reality
R acism does not exist
E ating healthily would only happen
A world with no hunting
M y perfect world.

Jamie Wharton (10)
Branston County Junior School, Branston

I Have A Dream!

I have a dream of a better place and this is how it goes,

H eroes saving days
A life when everyone is friendly
V iolence does not exist
E veryone has a house, money, food and water

A time of happiness

D ifferences are accepted
R acism is not thought about
E xtra-terrestrials live on the planet
A ll of the planets and stars are lived on
M ankind *doesn't* pollute
    That is my dream world.

Oliver Wake (9)
Branston County Junior School, Branston

Young Writers - I Have A Dream Reality Bites!

My Perfect World

When Earth was in a deep sleep
Uranus and Saturn were in an argument about who was the best
Then Jupiter awoke from his rest
Jupiter then shouted, 'Be quiet you two
Everyone is asleep except for you.'
Uranus turned round to Earth,
'I wish I was like him with all happy people living within.'
That would be a wonderful world
With happiness and peace
But when people are sad they can turn quite bad
So something can be done to make the world more fun
We can all work together and make peace last forever
So we can try and make my dream come true
Not just for me, but for other people too.

Chloe Souter (11)
Branston County Junior School, Branston

My Perfect World

In my perfect world where nobody is bad
There is no more fighting and everyone is glad.

In my perfect world where everyone is keen
To be kind to animals and not to be mean.

In my perfect world where everyone is healthy
There is no more sickness and everybody's wealthy.

In my perfect world where nothing can go wrong
I'm just beginning to realise we could have had it all along.

If we were all kind and everyone was fine
With people with different coloured skins the world would be divine.

Jed Willcox (11)
Branston County Junior School, Branston

The Complete Picture

I walked in the toy store one day
And I heard a strange muttering coming from a jigsaw
I opened the lid and the pieces had something to say.

'I don't like the corners,' said the middle
And the other middles agreed.
'I really hate the middles,' whispered the corners
Making sure nobody heard.

So I decided to take that box home
And build the jigsaw again and again
Then I left all the pieces alone
And I came back that evening after my tea
I broke up the jigsaw and put it back in the box
Then I heard the pieces say,
'I quite like the corners,'
'And I find that the middles look good put together!'

So smile at people in the street
And talk to them every now and then
Treat people as you would like to be treated
And let other people live life to the full
As well as you do.

Melissa Bush (11)
Branston County Junior School, Branston

Dream Of Mine

Life will be perfect, life will be fun,
Live life to the max and it shall be done
Dreams can be true if you make them true
If you have a go in everything you do
Make it happen at least have a go
Things will come naturally, soon it will show
Take care of your life
And life will take care of you.

Oliver Bentley (11)
Branston County Junior School, Branston

I Have A Dream

Life is what you make of it and that will always be true
So it will help you exit those dark days that you're coming through
So what, if people are superstars, footballers and millionaires
It doesn't matter that some are behind bars
It's you that you should worry about, to make you care
To follow your heart, that's the key
So be as quick as a dart and start your journey
Dreams, hopes and nightmares
Friends, family and pets, all of them are there
Yet all of them are good and bad, they'll never dampen in the wet
I wish that this world was a better place for both you and I
Where everyone has a friendly face and no bad emotions
                                          when people die
In my head that world is what I mentioned
It gave me new hope for this old battered Earth
And to change it for the one in my head
And all because I had a dream.

Nicholas Huxtable (11)
Branston County Junior School, Branston

My Dream

I have a dream of a perfect world
Where it doesn't matter if sometimes you get things wrong.

I have a dream of a perfect world
Where we can learn from our mistakes and achievements and dreams.

But it's just a dream, there's no perfect world
Where there's no hard choices or hurt.

If we could just accept people
My dream of a perfect world could come true.

Abi Davis (11)
Branston County Junior School, Branston

The World In My Dreams

T o become captain of England cricket team
H ealthy
E ssex cricket team win 20/20 Cup

W ealthy
O wn a season ticket to every Pro 40 match
R ich
L ive a long life
D reams can come true

I ntelligence everyone has
N o more global warming

M ake a galactic army to stop aliens invading
Y outh stays in everyone

D o good things for each other
R acism is no more
E veryone is helpful and kind
A nimals don't get killed
M ake world peace
S ave the world.

Sam Burnett (11)
Branston County Junior School, Branston

I Have A Dream

The dream of a perfect world
Where there's no anger or rage
The dream of no racism of poverty
The dream of everyone getting along with each other
The dream of a perfect world
Where they look in the mirror
The dream of no terrorism or hate between black and white
The dream of freedom and friends
The dream of no bullies and world peace
If you try you can succeed
Remember the first cut is the deepest.

Bethany Donaldson (11)
Branston County Junior School, Branston

My Wonderful World

M e and my family to have happiness
Y oung to grow strong and healthy

W icked people to become loving and kind
O bvious people that have no sadness
N o cruelty
D amaged trees to grow strong and healthy
E ndangered species to become less endangered
R ide happily through life
F ind new friends in life
U ntreated animals and people to have a longer life
L ove and treat people how you want to be treated

W onderful people that have no homes that deserve them
    to be given to them
O lder people to be put into decent homes
R eceive wonderful gifts from family and friends
L astly, if you see someone that needs help go and help them
D on't make this world a horrid place

If all this happened, maybe the world might be a better place.

Sophie Brown (11)
Branston County Junior School, Branston

My Perfect World

In my perfect world no one is mean but everyone is kind
Not hurting animals and that's the way it should be.

In my perfect world I want everyone to be happy, rich and have
                                            a long-lasting life
Where they can enjoy themselves.

In my perfect world I imagine a peaceful river
If it has waves the world has something wrong.

I imagine this perfect world
And this is how I want it to be, but it's all in my head.

Joe Robinson (11)
Branston County Junior School, Branston

Perfect World

M y perfect world
Y our perfect world

P erfect, perfect, perfect
E veryone to be happy
R acism to be stopped
F riends will be forever
E veryone will stay together
C ruelty to animals will be stopped
T his is what I call a perfect world

W orld to be happy
O r to be different
R eady to change
L ife as it is
D on't be selfish, this is a perfect world!

Eden Haytree (11)
Branston County Junior School, Branston

I Have A Dream

I have a dream that everyone is happy

H appy with themselves when they look in the mirror
A dream that there is no more need for war
V iolence no more in all of the nations
E verything peaceful, everything calm

A bsolutely no need for caution or need for alarm

D reams that all animals are safe and protected
R id of all hunters, rid of all poachers
E verybody with food to eat
A nd nobody starving, nobody weak
M y perfect world this place is
   This is where I want to live.

Ben Samways (11)
Branston County Junior School, Branston

Perfect World

M y perfect world
Y our perfect world

P erfect world
E veryone can be themselves
R iots can be stopped so stop them
F ights are the same
E veryone be themselves
C an you tell?
T his of course is the perfect world

W orld of happiness
O r world of cheerfulness
R eal friendship
L ive life to the full
D o your best but enjoy it.

Jade Lee (11)
Branston County Junior School, Branston

I Have A Dream

I have a dream that one day I will get a good job and be happy

H ate will no longer be
A nd Man will live in peace with nature
V andalism will be wrong and we will take care
E veryone will be in peace together

A nd animals will have their freedom

D reams can come true if you believe they can
R ubbish will no longer clutter the Earth
E veryone can change
A nd everyone is different
M any people have changed the world.

Gabriella Hill (10)
Branston County Junior School, Branston

Earth Cries

Each second a bleeding tear, each scene a blinding fear
Every sound a frightening scream, every sense a racing thought.
Life is no longer right, I have had not one sleeping night
Life is going so wrong, my enemy's now so strong.
My mind so weak, my thoughts so bleak
What is wrong with me?
Why can you not hear my misery?
Why do I
Have to scream so loud?
Just to be heard
At all?

I have overcome my last taste of humankind
Human is something that lives without pollution, electricity
They belong to that no more
My wounds are becoming more sore, my weakness bounding up
                                                      upon me
It hurts because it is getting much worse.
Dying is the first stage of life and to say it's different
For the Earth, well that would be a lie
It will be another to carry on, but it will never be what God made it.

Death, the first light I will see
Birth, the first death to dawn upon me
Death, that is not all.
Death is what is making our planet so small
So hopeless so vulnerable
I hate the idea of Earth's poor fate
Of what they do, everything so new
Earth is dying because of their faults, so the outside life will kill us
Kill us all, they have already killed themselves
I have a dream that Earth could once be a perfect place.

Frances Payne (11)
Branston County Junior School, Branston

My Perfect World

My perfect world is . . .
Where everyone is treated equal for who they are not what they do
And everyone has peace, love and happiness
Where people get along and animals have their freedom
Where there is no poverty, hate or wealth
Where everyone is there for each other and cares for each other
For us all to get along in a world of harmony with no war or terror
For everyone not to take their health for granted
And to be known for what we do, not what we have
That is my perfect world!

Lucia Brown (11)
Branston County Junior School, Branston

I Have A Dream

The world should live in peace
People *have* changed the world
Make the world *a* better place
I *dream* of a perfect world!

Amy Townsend (10)
Branston County Junior School, Branston

My Perfect World

If I had a dream
I'd need a theme like rapping or street scrapping
Every time I meet a rapper I shake his hand on demand
What's with east coast, west coast?
It's just we all have to boast
When I'm really mad I do something bad
Like get in a fight, turn off the light
And dream of my *perfect world!*

Danny Read (11)
Branston County Junior School, Branston

Very Big World

Paige woke up one morning
Her smile spread across her face
She put on her favourite clothes
And packed spares just in case.

She strode out of the front door
With her lunchbox filled to the brim
She walked past that old lady
Who lived out by the bins.

She saw a newspaper headline
'Attack Leaves Two Dead'
She smiled to herself
As thoughts of friends filled her head.

She saw a girl with a mirror
Her face as white as stone
Her eyes were filled with tears
But Paige, she just walked on.

Because in her head the world is perfect
She's healthy, popular and rich
It doesn't matter to her
That some people's worlds are in bits.

Because people hate themselves
And others just as much
And our planet's being destroyed
With fumes, gas and leftovers from people's lunch.

So everyone should be happy
Just like Paige, that girl
But just help others around you
And realise we live in a very big world.

Tia Wake (11)
Branston County Junior School, Branston

The Toy Box

Once walking in a market I saw a toy box,
It was red and green and blue and a bit of purple too.

When suddenly the toys inside began to argue,
'I don't like Bear,' said Doll.
Train said, 'Nor do I'
Spinning Top came along and this was his reply,
'We are a toy box that does not agree
If we don't act fast we might go on a madness spree!'

I took the toy box home and I began to play,
'Pay attention now and listen to what I say.'

Bear became a powerful king and Doll became Queen
The blocks became a castle and toy mice would sing

The train is now a carriage taking King down town
To buy his dear wife a lovely golden gown.

The toys are now all friends
And always help each other whenever there's a tricky bend.

Now this world is like a toy box, each of us unique
Thank you for listening to these words I love to speak.

Wade Garrett (11)
Branston County Junior School, Branston

Playing Fruit

One day a little grape was sat on the floor
The apple said, 'I'll play with you so you're not sad anymore.'
Then the banana came along,
'I don't want to play with you grape, you're too tiny
And as for you apple, you're too shiny.'
If everyone was like grape or apple
The world would be a much better place.

Amy Wallis (11)
Branston County Junior School, Branston

Life Would Be Perfect

Life would be perfect if I never lost
I'd own the world, I'd be the boss.

Life would be perfect if I could do anything
And I stood highest, taller than any king.

Life would be perfect if I knew everything without a doubt
And I could . . . wait maybe that is not what life's about.

Maybe I was wrong, wrong all along
Maybe I was selfish with this
Maybe life would be perfect
If we knew what a perfect life is.

Daniel Davis (11)
Branston County Junior School, Branston

I Have A Dream

I have a dream that the world was peaceful with no wars.
I have a dream that more people will support ICRF
So that they can continue with their great work.
I have a dream that whale hunting will stop
Then the wonderful creatures can still roam free.
I have a dream to see volcanoes erupt all around the world
From a safe distance
And for other people to be interested also.
I have a dream that more people will opt for geology
So I can help them explore its different aspects.
I have a dream for my family to be safe and happy
That everyone else will be happy too.
That's my dream.

Heather Booth (12)
Castle Rushen High School, Castletown

I Have A Dream

I have a dream that poverty will be history for good
And that there will be fairer trade in the world.
I have a dream.

I have a dream that more people will buy fair trade food
So that the producers can have a better life
I have a dream.

I have a dream that there will be peace in the world
And there will be no more wars
I have a dream.

I have a dream that all ivory hunting and animal cruelty will stop
And that for the future anyone who is found guilty of it is fined
I have a dream.

I have a dream that all my family will be safe and happy forever
I have a dream.

Lydia Harris (12)
Castle Rushen High School, Castletown

I Have A Dream . . .

I have a dream that an exploring ship will explore like me.
I have a dream that this ship will be called Marco Polo.
I have a dream that everyone will be a great explorer.
I have a dream that those who are too weak to explore
Will be told by the strong.
I have a dream that the poorest person will go on an adventure
I have a dream that this person will discover a land mass unknown
to Man.
I have a dream that the world will be a hive for explorers
I have a dream that the world will be united by the compass
I have a dream that no one will tell a lie and everyone will be a believer.

Chloe Sullivan (12)
Castle Rushen High School, Castletown

I Have A Dream

I have a dream . . .
That richer countries will help poorer countries.

I have a dream . . .
That poorer countries will have enough money to buy resources.

I have a dream . . .
That poorer countries have enough money to buy food and water.

I have a dream . . .
That we can help build hospitals to keep people alive.

I have a dream . . .
That poorer people can live just like richer people do.

I have a dream . . .
That poor people will have real houses to go home to at night.

I have a dream . . .
That we, together, can make poverty history!

Philip Cringle (12)
Castle Rushen High School, Castletown

I Have A Dream

I have a dream to train and train to be the best in the world.
I have a dream to set off at lightning speed when I hear the sound
of the pistol.
I have a dream to sprint for my life.
I have a dream to make England see that I am a top athlete.
I have a dream to run like a cheetah and have the wind racing
through my hair.
I have a dream to beat my personal best and for everyone to know
I am a champion.
I have a dream to set a world record
I have a dream to *win!*

Katie Gilson (12)
Castle Rushen High School, Castletown

I Have A Dream

I have a dream that people will respect musicians who are long dead
That the founders of all music shall have as much respect as Oasis
or James Blunt.

I have a dream that people may enjoy music written 200 years ago
As well as music written last month.
That music of different styles such as baroque, classical, romantic
Impressionist and modern may be enjoyed

I have a dream that even with all the modern bands, orchestras
will be revered and loved
That people will enjoy seeing it on television, if not in person.

I have a dream that the older music will be loved and enjoyed
Like it was before modern music
I have a dream!

Terence Lennon (11)
Castle Rushen High School, Castletown

I Have A Dream

I have a dream that I will run like a magic cheetah
With all the wind brushing against my face.

I have a dream that I will be the first person to cross the line
And as I cross the line I will hear the crowd cheer and scream for me.

I have a dream that I will train to be the best and train to win.
I have a dream that my friends will see me run as fast as I can.

I have a dream that I will run faster than I have ever run before
I have a dream that my legs will win me a cup
And that my arms will win me the pride of a winner!

Abigail Swayne (12)
Castle Rushen High School, Castletown

I Have A Dream

I have a dream
That every child will have their rights and aren't treated badly.

I have a dream
That every child will be able to do the sport they want to do.

I have a dream
That France will win the World Cup again.

I have a dream
That all racism will stop and come to an end.

I have a dream
That Arsenal will get even better and will win everything.

I have a dream
That Zinadine Zidane will not retire and stay with France.

I have a dream
That all people will be as passionate as French people.

Zack Skuszka (12)
Castle Rushen High School, Castletown

I Have A Dream

I have a dream that I can help teach others to be champions
So that anyone who has a dream to sprint will win.
I have a dream that I will live to see future Olympics
And feel that atmosphere in the stadium again.
I have a dream that I will see the Olympic flame again
To experience that united feeling and understand the sense
of achievement.
I have a dream to be filled up with that amazing feeling of happiness,
once more

I have a dream to win again.

Catreeney Harkin (12)
Castle Rushen High School, Castletown

Arnold Schwarzenegger

I have a dream
A dream that I have a shorter surname.

I have a dream
A dream that people will stop smoking.

I have a dream
A dream that James Cameron directed Terminator 3.

I have a dream
A dream that people will decide to get fit.

I have a dream
A dream that people don't die in cars.

I have a dream
A dream that we can make a bio-friendly diesel engine.

I have a dream
A dream, that actors can become the President of America.

I have a dream
A dream that I can be number 1 actor in the world!

Thomas Richardson Hall (11)
Castle Rushen High School, Castletown

I Have A Dream

I have a dream that I will get a perfect 10
That I will win the Olympics
To inspire people to do gymnastics.
I have a dream that everybody will enjoy the sport of gymnastics
That I will coach a group of perfect gymnasts
That people will watch it on TV if they can't see it live.
I have a dream that people will achieve a high standard
That everyone will have equal coaching so there are no favourites
I have a dream.

Kayleigh Masson (12)
Castle Rushen High School, Castletown

I Have A Dream

I have a dream that girls and boys will play football
                                    professionally together
That they will be seen as equals by the crowds and everyone
                                              else watching.
I have a dream that one day I will be able to help girls all over the world
Play the beautiful game, that I can teach them to use skills and dribble
As well as any professional man.
I have a dream that my team Everton will beat Charlton
And Arsenal in the Premiership
That one day our team will have new young players
That have put their lives to football just as we have.
I have a dream that in years to come there will be hundreds
Of girl soccer schools set up to find girls with natural talent
That I and my team will lift the World Cup.

Ruby Callister (12)
Castle Rushen High School, Castletown

I Have A Dream

I have a dream that younger people shall have fun playing football.
That I shall teach how to play it well and with honour.
I have a dream that they shall not argue over it
That it will not cause arguments.
I have a dream that it shall be played for fun
That people will get along.

I have a dream that there will be no poor people
That there will be no starvation.
I have a dream that I'll raise money for the poor
That we shall all be equal.
I have a dream that everyone shall have equal shares of money
That there will be no more poor or starving people.

Tom Bowden (12)
Castle Rushen High School, Castletown

Steven Gerrard

I have a dream that people will play football, black or white
That there won't be any more racism from fans anywhere.
I have a dream that people play fairly with no bad fouls,
That people get paid the same amount each week.
I have a dream that nobody cheats at football
That academies accept poor people without enough money to have
their chance at a job.
I have a dream that referees will not dismiss people
That people don't play for fame and glory or money.
I have a dream that people play because it is their passion
That players play for the support of the fans.
I have a dream that Liverpool are the last team in Europe
That they win the Champions League five times in a row.
I have a dream that teams don't get criticised
That managers don't get sacked because of lack of progress.
I have a dream that people won't want to leave a club in a lower league
That people will stay loyal to their club even if they
have been relegated.
I have a dream that my dream will come true.

Kieran Tildesley (12)
Castle Rushen High School, Castletown

I Have A Dream

I have a dream that one day all children will be adventurous.
I have a dream that one day the world will be full of adventure.
I have a dream that one day there will be no villains.
I have a dream that one day all children will have gadgets.
I have a dream that one day the world will all be good.
I have a dream that one day all children will be like James Bond.
I have a dream that one day all children will look for adventure.
I have a dream.

Harry Harrison (12)
Castle Rushen High School, Castletown

I Have A Dream

I have a dream that racism will be kicked out of football
That no more things will be thrown at footballers.

I have a dream that cheating will be banished
That no more diving will occur in a match.

I have a dream that Brazil will win another World Cup
That all the Brazilians will triumph over all.

I have a dream that I will win another player of the year award
That I will play with flair and passion
To show people what Joga Bonito really means.

Patrick Gandy (11)
Castle Rushen High School, Castletown

I Have A Dream

I have a dream that all children will enjoy and read books
That children will never be sad, poor or hungry.
I have a dream that people will get their imaginations back
                                        through books.
That all children are given fair chances and education.
I have a dream!
I have a dream that all races and classes of people
Will be treated the same and given the same chance
I have a dream that books will be treated with more respect.

Ferghal Clucas-Morris (12)
Castle Rushen High School, Castletown

I Have A Dream

I have a dream that I will win the 2006 and 2007 Grand Prix
That my career with McLaren will be very successful.
I have a dream that I become the next Juan Fangio
That they will make new tracks to test my skill.
I have a dream that someone will invent a car that will corner better
That can reach higher top speeds and engines that don't overheat.
I have a dream that my son will become what I am,
That he will follow in my footsteps to triumph.
I have a dream that they will make better tyre compounds
That they will put active suspension on the cars but still be lightweight.

Blaine Perston (12)
Castle Rushen High School, Castletown

I Have A Dream

I have a dream that I will be a gymnast.
That I will get to be in the Olympics.
I have a dream that I will get a perfect 10.
I have a dream that I will only be young
I have a dream I will be a coach
And have a group that will get a perfect 10
And become a coach themselves.
I have a dream that people will achieve the standard I did
And the children will be coached the same so there are no favourites
I have a dream, I have a dream.

Bethany Quayle (11)
Castle Rushen High School, Castletown

I Have A Dream

I have a dream that people will be accepted.
I have a dream that people can be free from slavery.
I have a dream that ideas can be accepted.
I have a dream that people enjoy their jobs.
I have a dream that friends stick together.
I have a dream that people can live without conflict and war
I have a dream.

Daniel Price (12)
Castle Rushen High School, Castletown

I Have A Dream

I have a dream to change the world
To change the bad things to good,
To stop all wars and make people equal
So that everyone can be understood.

I have a dream to change the world
To change the bad things to good,
To stop all murders so most people live
Until the end of adulthood.

I have a dream to change the world
To change the bad things to good,
To stop all bullies giving people abuse
Like the nice people would.

I have a dream to change the world
To change the bad things to good,
To stop all the people being racist
And carry on as we should.

I have a dream to change the world
To change the bad things to good,
So that everyone can live in peace
And then there's no need for Robin Hood.

Kirsty Lane (13)
De Ferrers Technology College, Burton upon Trent

I Have A Dream

I have a dream . . .
That everyone will be as talented as Beethoven
He's my inspiration
He's what makes me want to play the piano.

I have a dream . . .
That everyone will be kind as my grandma
A smile for each person
Not a bad word to say about anyone near or far.

I have a dream . . .
That everyone will be as brave as the army
Some think they're barmy
Only if barmy means putting others first.

I have a dream . . .
That everyone will be as lucky as me
For me, my family would cut off their knee
If you don't have one of the bad diseases you are lucky.

I have a dream . . .
That racism will end
Everyone will be seen as equals
Because racism's driving me round the bend.

These are my dreams
They should be easy
Just a little communication
To stop us feeling this frustration.

Chloe Bayston (13)
De Ferrers Technology College, Burton upon Trent

My Hockey Team Poem

One night, I had a dream
That I was in a hockey team,
But some of the players were different to me,
On the pitch it was plain to see.

Some were black, some were white,
All were ranging in weight and height,
Some from China, some from Japan,
The way they looked - there was no ban.

Every player had a touch of the ball,
No one was left out or bullied at all,
We realised it was an *equal* game,
In *every* way, everyone was the same.

So, I have a dream that I hope comes true,
So life's enjoyed by me and you,
That all racism and bullying ends,
Upon countries of the world this depends.

Think about other lives today,
Let those people have their say,
We're on this Earth as one big team,
In peace and harmony, that's my dream.

Jenny Heathcote (13)
De Ferrers Technology College, Burton upon Trent

Changed For Good

A world with peace and happiness
Love and care, equality
Laughter in the air around
Smiles big and proud.

Crying in the gutter now
Is all the bad and evil
The crown of bad has changed for good
The black blanket has been lifted.

Emily Moss (13)
De Ferrers Technology College, Burton upon Trent

This Is Our Dream

Walking through a world of peace
I have a dream
Walking through a world of growth
I have a dream
Walking through a world of wealth
I have a dream
Walking through a world of water
I have a dream
Walking through a world of health
I have a dream
Walking through a world of care
I have a dream
Walking through a world of happiness
I have a dream

Walking through a world of war
This is no dream
Walking through a world of famine
This is no dream
Walking through a world of poverty
This is no dream
Walking through a world of drought
This is no dream
Walking through a world of illness
This is no dream
Walking through a world of crime
This is no dream
Walking through a world of sadness
This is no dream.

Elina Baker & Emily Moss (13)
De Ferrers Technology College, Burton upon Trent

The World Is Words

The world is words,
The world is woe,
The world is peace,
The world is foe.

The world is smooth,
The world is dreams,
The world is never,
What is seems.

The world is run,
The world is walk,
The world is whisper,
The world is talk.

The world is round,
The world's a ball,
The world is words,
To change us all.

Christopher Moss (13)
De Ferrers Technology College, Burton upon Trent

Why Is There Racism In The World?

Don't judge people by the colour of their skin
Everyone is different by what they believe in.

Black, yellow, white or brown
Why is there racism to bring us down?
Racism is unfair and nobody wants it in the air!
Stop racism!

The perfect world
I would like to have lived in
With no racism, not feeling ashamed
To walk out the door.

Nadia Saghir (12)
De Ferrers Technology College, Burton upon Trent

Racism

There is racism everywhere
Can it stop there?
It's between black and white
So stop this stupid fight.

Problems can be solved by talking
So stop the stalking
And stop the war
Because that's what a treaty is for.

This fight is very strange
So stop getting your guns in range
So please stop this
And restore harmony and bliss.

Who will we send
To make this end?
We will not be defeated
So please be seated.

Daniel Jones (12)
De Ferrers Technology College, Burton upon Trent

Racism

It doesn't matter if we're black or white
We are all the same
This is no game.
It doesn't matter if we're black or white
No one is perfect and always right.
Racism is evil and shouldn't be allowed
So what if we're different and stand out from the crowd
Wars, blood, violence and crime
What's happening in this world of mine?
Let's all join together and be happy, not sad
Just think of all the good times that can be had
Forget about religion and colour of skin
Everyone has a right to live in the world we're in!

Mariam Begum (12)
De Ferrers Technology College, Burton upon Trent

Racism

Why are we mean to people who are black?
We're all one race, all one pack.

Together we can make the world just right
Instead of making wars and always trying to fight.

Just even thinking it makes me sad
Of how we can be this mad, so bad.

Imagine if this world was a much better place
We'd be going round singing, we're all the human race!

There's racism everywhere all over the USA
What can we do? We don't have a say.

Even if you're black, white or somewhere in-between
There's always some hate, the worst thing I've ever seen.

So everyone out there, please hear me out
Try to sort this, what's it all about?

Rachel Freeman (11)
De Ferrers Technology College, Burton upon Trent

I Have A Dream

I have a dream where we would all care
We weren't superficial, we'd all learned to share.

We didn't judge people by the way they appeared
Nobody worried and they never feared.

Maybe this dream could soon be real
If we all could love; if we all could feel.

Then I had a dream of terror and hate
Everyone was an enemy, no one was a mate.

It was then that I found, perfect we sought
Perhaps the world's not as bad as everyone thought.

The world's getting better, we are on our way
Not quite there yet, but we're getting there, eh?

Daniel Carter (13)
De Ferrers Technology College, Burton upon Trent

I Have A Dream

I have a dream
No more racism

I have a dream
No more war

I have a dream

I have a dream
No more poverty

I have a dream
No more murder

I have a dream

I have a dream
No more animal cruelty

I have a dream
No more abuse to children

I have a dream

These are my words to change the world.

Emily Lakin (13)
De Ferrers Technology College, Burton upon Trent

Racism

It ain't about if you're black or white
Just so long as you can be pure to see the light.

But in society it's very hard to find
A certain equality that's in the heart divine.

Mr Luther King was a one of a kind
He believed in the people and their fragile minds.

Black people getting shot on the streets
One together that's how our hearts should beat.

The people don't get the chance for the shouts
But we're all human beings with rights *peace out!*

Liam Anguish (12)
De Ferrers Technology College, Burton upon Trent

Racism!

Why is racism going on?
We're all equal.
Why does it matter where we're from?
We all deserve an even chance.

Why isn't everyone treated the same?
Everyone is different.
Why aren't we happy more people came?
Just because of different skin colours.

Why are we being bullied?
No one is better than others.
Just because we're different coloured
Can't it be perfect where . . .

People coloured black or white,
We're all the same inside.
Why are people seen in a different light?
Stop racism right now!

Louisa Statham (12)
De Ferrers Technology College, Burton upon Trent

I Have A Dream

I is for inequality, as we act as if we are right

H is for horror, because we kill people for what we think
A is for afterwards, because we think *after* we do wrong
V is for violence which we use on other nations
E is for evil which racism spreads worldwide

A is for ages, which have had the same problem

D is for dreamland where racism doesn't exist
R is for racism which this poem is about
E is for equal which is what everyone is
A is for a reason which we don't have for murder
M is for Martin Luther King who died for making peace.

Jack Roberts (12)
De Ferrers Technology College, Burton upon Trent

Racism

Now this is a poem all about how
My life got flipped, turned upside down
And now if you wanna hear my poem
Just sit right there and I'll tell you
About my time in London's Mayfair.

It's my first time in London
Starting a new job
Just turned down a street
Gettin' stalked by a mob.

They caught up with me
Dissing the colour of my skin
I tried to make them stop
But there's no way I could win.

I survived that day
Hoping for another
I'd cry out for help
Especially to my mother.

We are filled with lots of fear
Every day throughout the year
I want it to stop
Cos I don't want my plea to end in a flop
Stop racism now!

John O'Brien (12)
De Ferrers Technology College, Burton upon Trent

Racism

I'm writing a poem about racism
For all the wars that we have
Black and white people are all the same
We all breathe in the same air and live on the same Earth
People should all get along and not fight because of their colour
So stop racism!

Shane Gregory (12)
De Ferrers Technology College, Burton upon Trent

Domestic Violence

Dear diary
Today I met a man, he really understands me,
He listens to me, he really gets me.
I hope I get to know him.

Dear diary,
I've known him for two weeks
And things are turning sour.
He shouts at me and sometimes hits me,
I don't want to know him anymore.

Dear diary
It's been four weeks . . .
I'm not enjoying this at all.
The punches are more frequent,
He shouts at me, we never talk at all.

Dear diary,
This time he's gone too far,
He hit me round the head.

Dear diary,
I am dead
All I hope is, is that my story
Will save the lives of thousands of women.

Joe Wheeler (13)
De Ferrers Technology College, Burton upon Trent

I Have A Dream

A dream of mine has always been
To see a stream where love has been
And to drink the water from that stream;
So that I can have love of peace and make peace reality.

I have a dream, I have a dream.

Harrison Collins (12)
De La Salle College, St Saviour

The Peace Of The World!

The peace of the world is my dream
Where wars never started
Guns never existed
And bombs were never built.

My dream of a world without racism
Nobody cares about what colour you are
No one notices what religion you follow
And no one goes hungry.

My dream of a world without poverty
When money is never needed
When food is equally shared
And water is everywhere.

My dream of a world where violence was never discovered
Abuse is destroyed
Hunting is cut down for good
Animals aren't killed needlessly.

We are all equal, we all deserve a fun
Happy, loving world without anger, hate and sorrow.

Miles Thompson (12)
De La Salle College, St Saviour

I Have A Dream

I have a dream of a world in which everything's fair,
Where it does not matter whether you're black or white,
A world where it does not matter, you still care,
And everything is united no matter what your colour.

Where the rivers flow with true love and joy,
Where the streets are full of kindness and true friendship,
Where the difference does not matter,
Everybody is treated the same.

Frederick Kelleher (12)
De La Salle College, St Saviour

I Have A Dream

One dream is a dream for everyone
People have dreams that won't come true
Some have dreams that are weird
If you keep on dreaming your dream may come true.

Dreams are remembered during the night
That's when people dream, long into the night
Some dreams are the same, some are not
During dreams you should feel the best
So dream on!

Charles Hubert (12)
De La Salle College, St Saviour

I Have A Dream

I have a dream that the world is perfectly free,
That black and white don't matter when people see,
I have a dream that religion and sex don't affect this land,
And the world will join together, hand in hand.

I have a dream that the world will work together as a team
And destroy poverty, that's my *dream!*

Alexander Mayes (12)
De La Salle College, St Saviour

Dreams

D reams of meadows with soft grass,
R abbits and hamsters by me pass
E merald leaves of trees up high
A nimals with wonders enough to make you fly
M eals and money make the world go buy
S apphire seas now taste like pie.

Robin Martins (12)
De La Salle College, St Saviour

I Have A Dream

I have a dream of worldwide peace
No murder, no drugs, no rape, no poverty.

I dream of a multicultural world
One that accepts someone for who they are
Not a world of judging from the colour of one's skin.

I dream of equality, so all people
Black or white can enjoy the same things together

I dream also of a world free of crime
To help my dream of worldwide peace.

Louis Richardson (12)
De La Salle College, St Saviour

I Have A Dream

I have a dream that money is shared equally,
I have a dream that all people, great and small, get treated the same,
The candy tree will feed the world,
I have a dream that children don't have chores,
I have a dream that peace strikes all the nations and war will be
                                                        no more.

David Jolley (12)
De La Salle College, St Saviour

I Have A Dream

I have a dream that my family will win the lottery
And that money grows on trees!
I have a dream that there is peace in the world
And that moss turns into candyfloss
I have a dream!

Mitchell Dellar-Crone (12)
De La Salle College, St Saviour

I Have A Dream

God may have created the world,
But it sure isn't perfect,
With violence and inequality.

If it is like this it might as well be mist,
But this is no reason to start using your fists.

With racism and hatred,
Being the wrong way to go,
Is this the right example to show?

While there is war and destruction at this awful time,
There is peace and creation while writing this rhyme.

In time of war people live in dread
And they are afraid to get out of bed.

We'd better stop now, before it's too late,
Otherwise we will all suffer a fate.

Chris Bellot (13)
De La Salle College, St Saviour

I Have A Dream

I have a dream . . .
That friends and foes shall be no more
And we will live in a world where war is just a fantasy.

Never to be in a world that won't be governed by you or me
But by all people, black and white
From all corners of the globe
Working together, making the world a better place
Stamping out the evil and encouraging the good
But alas, in the end I know this is but a faraway dream.

George Eddie (12)
De La Salle College, St Saviour

Peace

I have a dream to remove all crime
No hate between families
No muggings in the street
No violence between each other.

I have a dream to banish all poverty
No hunger between children
No sexual abuse
No diseases that can't be cured.

I have a dream to get rid of bullies
No picking on little kids
No kicking in the classrooms
No teasing behind the bike sheds.

Aaron Labey (13)
De La Salle College, St Saviour

I Have A Dream

I have a dream of a world so clean
With money growing on trees
Where poverty is not at large
And famine is extinct.

I have a dream
That colour's not what makes a man
And personality is what does
But what I hope for most of all
Is everyone is equal.

Aaron Quinlan (12)
De La Salle College, St Saviour

I Have A Dream

I have a dream that I'm on top of the world.
I have a dream that I'm number one.
I have a dream
That everyone is different.
I have a dream
That the world can change from bad to good.
I have a dream
That no one in the world will live in poverty.
I have a dream
That everyone in the world will get a good job.
I have a dream
That when people die they will live happily in Heaven.
I have a dream
That everyone will recycle.
I have a dream that I will have a very pretty wife.
I had a cool dream, that's my dream over
Thanks for listening.

Stephen Le Brun (14)
De La Salle College, St Saviour

I Have A Dream

I have a dream to have a big manor house.
I have a dream to have a family.
I have a dream to have a Bugatti Veron.
I have a dream to make people smile.
I have a dream to direct a film.
I have a dream to write an adventure book.
I have a dream to see no poverty in the world.
I have a dream that all people will be equal.
I have a dream that global warming will stop.
I have a dream to have my own Boeing 747
I have a dream that me, my family and friends will live forever.
I have a dream to lift the World Cups in football and rugby.

Anthony Regan (14)
De La Salle College, St Saviour

The Winning Shot

The winning shot
As I was standing on the tee
Thinking to myself, *the winner could be me*
The pressure was on, thinking to myself, *is this club wrong?*
Placed my ball upon the tee knowing that there was only
one chance for me
I got in the position to take the shot, now the heat was on
I was really hot
I took my club back then I hit the ball with a lot of force,
It was flying down the course
The ball came down like a flare
The ball was on the green, now I was halfway there
I walked up the fairway thinking to myself, *it's all right, everything
will be OK*
I took my putter out of my bag
This is it, the winning shot, I thought to myself
I hit the ball along the line, it went in the hole, now the championship
was mine.
This is my dream!

Jason Higgins (14)
De La Salle College, St Saviour

I Have A Dream

I have a dream that I can eat a big ice cream.
I have a dream that I make my sister scream.
I have a dream that I will be the greatest football player.
I have a dream that I will be a saviour.
I have a dream that I am on top of the world.
I have a dream that there is peace in the entire world.
I have a dream that I can fly.
I have a dream that I will never die.
I have a dream that I will have the greatest wife.
I have a dream that I will have a funny and full life.

Alexander Carpenter (14)
De La Salle College, St Saviour

World Peace

I have a dream
My dream is to stop poverty
Come with me now
To help people with no property.

It's not about skins
It's about love and peace
Now listen to this
Because this is my speech.

We all want peace
To stop racism too
Now all come with me
To stop poverty too.

Ciaran Tyrrell (11)
De La Salle College, St Saviour

I Have A Dream!

I have a dream
That is like a stream
It carries on down towards the sea
It spreads the joy around the world
Sending good news from that word
Not Hell, not hatred, yes, peace.

Heller Garcia (12)
De La Salle College, St Saviour

I Have A Dream

I have a dream
That one day the pollution stops
And doesn't kill the bunny that hops.

The forests are filled with gigantic trees
And not chopped down by men as they please.

We stop the innocent men being slain
And free the world of all the pain.

World hunger and poverty stops in a flash
And they have food like bangers and mash.

If we free the world of all racism,
We can have a place which is a world worth living in.

James Chan (12)
Elizabeth College, St Peter Port

I Have A Dream

I have a dream
That one day justice will come
And not be taken away.

No more terrorism or street crime
Justice will rule and end most fights.

With no machine guns and hand grenades
Justice will rule, crime will end
The Mafia will fall.

Iraq will be unified
Guatanemo Bay will crumble
With an almighty rumble
Dictatorship will have died.

James Firth (12)
Elizabeth College, St Peter Port

I Have A Dream

I have a dream . . .
No war, no poverty, no hate,
I dream of a day where this becomes true,
But it is just a dream
Just a dream . . .

I have a dream . . .
I am the richest, I am the best, I beat the rest,
I dream of a day where this becomes true,
But it is just a dream
Just a dream . . .

I have a dream . . .
No pollution, no animals dying, no litter,
I dream of a day where this becomes true,
But it is just a dream
Just a dream . . .

I have a dream . . .
My friends, my family live forever
I dream of a day where all these things happen,
But it is still just a dream,
Just a long, long dream . . .

Nathanial Eker (11)
Elizabeth College, St Peter Port

I Have A Dream That Some Day . . .

I have a dream that some day
People will all share joy

I have a dream that some day
People will have peace

I have a dream that some day
There will be peace

I have a dream that some day
Everyone will be happy

I have a dream that some day
Racism will be abolished

I have a dream that some day
Poverty will be solved

I have a dream that some day
World hunger will be no more

I have a dream that some day
Governments will not be corrupt

I have a dream that some day
Those without homes will have one

I have a dream that some day
Those uneducated will learn.

Nicholas Harris (13)
Elizabeth College, St Peter Port

I Have A Dream

I have a dream,
That we all knew
Why it is we're put here,
That we could start anew.

All of mankind's errors
Are resting on our chest
And all of this world's treasures
Are guarded by our best.

With all the politicians
Dictating our lives,
Shouting their care from rooftops,
Turning a blind eye.

Jesus dead on the cross,
Us to Heaven send,
Now with all our bloodshed,
Our pain will never end.

Nicholas Kerins (12)
Elizabeth College, St Peter Port

I Have A Dream

I have a dream that some day I can fly,
Up high through the clouds in the sky,
I have a dream that countries can live in peace
And not have a war at every little argument.

I have a dream that diseases are no more
And that people only die by old age,
I have a dream that people do not steal,
They work to earn the privilege to have it.

I have a dream that people do not break rules,
That people listen and respect others' opinions,
I have a dream that all races get along
And people do not die of starvation.

Ryan Ferbrache (12)
Elizabeth College, St Peter Port

I Have A Dream . . .

I have a dream that one day everyone will be friendly towards
each other,
No arguing, quarrelling or fighting each other.
The disputes and differences talked about,
Equality for everyone, let's shout!
I have a dream like no other.

Religion, who we worship, let's not argue,
We are all different, that we know.
There is room for everyone to pray,
Yes, we can all have our say.
I have a dream to share with you.

Black and white, there is no difference,
The only thing that differs is our appearance.
Our feelings are all the same,
There should be no reason to hide in shame.
I have a dream we all need patience.

We are all alike, rich or poor,
Why continue bickering? No more!
Let's help the countries that need us,
We should stop making such a fuss.
I have a dream, let's stop this war!

I have a dream, life will be fair to all,
Everyone will get along, it's a tough call.
But, we will succeed if we all try,
To pull together and hear me cry,
I have a dream . . .

Jean-Pierre Payne (12)
Elizabeth College, St Peter Port

I Have A Dream

I have a dream,
Free us,
Free us,
What have we done
To deserve this?

Free us,
Free us,
What do we have different from you?
We are all made the same,
We are all equal.

Free us,
Free us,
Stop attacking us, let us be free,
Let us be free so black and white can join hands.

Free us,
Free us,
Let us play with white people,
Let us laugh and joke together.

Free us,
Free us,
I have a dream today.

Henry Carre (13)
Elizabeth College, St Peter Port

I Have A Dream

I have a dream
A world free of pollution,
A world free of poverty,
A world free of disease.

I have a dream
Let us be free,
Let us be free,
Give it to us.

A world free of weapons,
A world free of discrimination,
A world free of evil souls.

I have a dream
Let us be free,
Let us be free,
Give it to us,
Give it to us, please.

Alex Wilson (13)
Elizabeth College, St Peter Port

I Have A Dream

I have a dream that all people can be free of all troubles in the world
And that they will all learn from each other.
They will be able to forget their worries
And have a life of peace.
They'll live in harmony,
All the wars will cease.

I have a dream that all children won't be hurt,
That adults won't abuse and spoil their lives.
All races will get along
And all sing the same song.
All religions will see,
That everyone can agree.

Alex Lacey (12)
Elizabeth College, St Peter Port

I Have A Dream

I have a dream that the sun will rise to view a different world.

A world without pollution,
A world without suffering, and
A world without drugs or gangs.

I have a dream that the newborn will live to see a different world.

A world without violence,
A world without hunger, and
A world where we respect each other.

I have a dream that the stars will witness a different world.

A world without poverty,
A world without disease, and
A world where we are all equal.

I have a dream that the animals around will live in a different world.

A world where we are closer to nature,
A world with clean air, and
A world where we can live peacefully.

Michael Hart (13)
Elizabeth College, St Peter Port

I Have These Dreams, Just These Dreams And Nothing More

I dream one day warfare shall cease, just this dream
                                    and nothing more.
I dream one day poverty shall end, just this dream and nothing more.
I dream one day hunger shall finally finish, just this dream
                                    and nothing more.
I dream one day humans will leave nature be, just this dream
                                    and nothing more.
I dream one day that people who didn't deserve to die do not,
Just this dream and nothing more.

Josh Cutter (13)
Elizabeth College, St Peter Port

I Have A Dream

I have a dream that people could agree,
Dreams become reality.

I have a dream that laws aren't broken,
Drugs not taken.

I have a dream that pollution can stop,
And nobody rules at the top.

I have a dream that animals aren't killed,
Their habitat is not destroyed.

I have a dream that people can be treated the same
And that no one is to blame.

I have a dream that poverty ends
Making the world just splendid.

I have a dream that wars will end,
So we could make up and all be friends.

Dreams are to be made real,
So let's help each other to achieve this aim.

Elliot R Clark (13)
Elizabeth College, St Peter Port

All You Want

When all you want is to live,
But can't find the time,
When all you want is love,
But can't find the one,
When all you want is to think,
But can't find the thoughts.
When all you want is to laugh,
But can't find the humour,
When all you want is everything,
You're asking too much.

Katie Prest (14)
Farnborough School Technology College, Clifton

A Past Memory

What would life be like if there was no me and you?
Would the whole universe crack straight in two?
Would our friendship fall apart?
And would we have to make a new start?
When you're there, I feel whole
And when you're not it tears apart my soul.
When we're together you make me laugh,
And when I'm alone I go a lonely path,
If I'd suffered a stressful day,
You'd always guide me along the way
And then at night we say goodbye
And I hear your voice
Your loving, caring, graceful voice
It gives my mind no choice
And as my eyes close shut
I think inside my head
Love is like
A roller coaster, so many ups and downs
But I know how much you love me and you'll always be around
So to all those people out there
Remember the ones who care
Friendship is one thing
Love is another
Nothing is stronger than mother and daughter
But when you were lonely, feeling blue,
Always remember I was here for you
So don't forget . . .
Love isn't always a boy and a girl,
It doesn't have to be all whirls and twirls
It can be between everyone and anything
Anyplace and everywhere
Anytime!

Holly Brindley & Paula Lydamore (13)
Farnborough School Technology College, Clifton

Cities' Streets

Have you ever drifted the alleys of cities' streets?
Have you ever gazed the streets at night when no one
Can be bothered to shed a little kindness?

Cities' streets at the horror of night when the alleys
Are crawling with people who have no home
Has it ever crossed your selfish computer to think of those
Who have no home?

I believe in an era when everyone definitely will have a place to stay,
When this will happen I do not know.

Something I do know is this will only take place
When the world is devoured and creatures
Recognise how lucky they are.

Cities' streets at the terror of night,
When the alleys are crawling with people who have no home,
Has it ever beseeched your facetious computer to think of those
Who have no home?

'We will not know what will happen in the future for sure,
But what we predict we can change by doing something about
it today.'

Anthony Leeming (15)
Farnborough School Technology College, Clifton

School Life

When you're young, live life to the full
Because in the meantime things will seem dull,
Work hard at school and don't be a fool,
Don't start smoking because you don't look cool,
Be nice to teachers, they are there to help you,
Don't show off and try to argue,
Try your hardest and always aim high,
Don't be stupid and try to lie,
When finally your day is done,
You can go out and have some fun.

Zak Thresher (13)
Farnborough School Technology College, Clifton

Depression

Look! and gaze into the mirror
As you look at your physique
Reflect! on the fact you are unique
No matter what others may say
You have companions, that is all that matters

Don't! waste your time in your chamber,
Thinking that no one is concerned,
Remember! what you've achieved and the respect you've gained.

There's a chance for everyone in life,
You go ahead, you blow that chance
No turning back, no second chance
Just one mistake, that's all it takes
To blow your life, it's all down the drain.

Your life is like a new page,
Fresh bedding, a beautiful wedding.

It's easy to throw away chances
Sit down through dances
Play safe avoid choices
Ignore your inner voices.

Don't look through beauty magazines,
As you will only think that you are ugly,
As you see those models posing smugly.

But trust me, on yourself . . .

James Colagiovanni (14)
Farnborough School Technology College, Clifton

Life

The way I see life is very straight forward
I see it as a piggy bank
The more you put in
The more you get out

Some people work hard for their money
But others steal and commit petty crimes
Some people become famous
And sing catchy lyrical rhymes

Some people go to college
And study real hard
Some people waste their lives
Watching TV eating lard.

Some people go to university,
A top rank place,
But others who don't even go to school,
Don't even know how to tie their lace.

The message I'm trying to give you,
Is to live your life to the full,
We all want a happy life,
Nothing boring or dull.

So remember,
If you contribute to your piggy bank
Your life will be full of joy
But if you don't put anything in
Your life will be empty
You won't be known as anything
Just another girl or boy.

Deneesh McDonald (14)
Farnborough School Technology College, Clifton

A Wonderful World

The sunset sinks slowly,
Behind the magnificent mountains.

The moon glistens balancing,
On the top of the hilltops.

Everyday the sun rises,
Everyday the sun sets.
This is our world.
A wonderful world,
A wonderful world.

The stars sparkle like glitter,
On a black piece of paper.

The birds sleeping snug in their beds,
Waiting for the early hours of the morning.

Everyday the sun rises,
Everyday the sun sets.
This is our world,
A wonderful world,
A wonderful world.

The tranquillity of the water flowing,
Soothes the heart of the night.

The hooting of the owls,
Sends shivers down the night's spine.

Everyday the sun rises,
Everyday the sun sets,
This is our world,
A wonderful world,
A wonderful world.

Oceans deep scatter across the world,
Sways among the beach.

As the morning comes,
The sun fills up the skies.

Everyday the sun rises,
Everyday the sun sets,
This is our world,
A wonderful world,
A wonderful world.

As the day drifts by,
The moon glistens once again.

Summoning the world to bed.

Michelle Bull & Laura Spencer (14)
Farnborough School Technology College, Clifton

I Have A Dream

I sit and cry through the night
As my whole life just passes by

I have so much trouble,
My life's in a muddle,
My life's a state,
I'm full of hate.

I need a friend to cuddle,
Not the ones that tear my bubble.

I want a friend, who's kind and polite,
Who puts things right,
I need a friend that cares,
A friend that always shares.

But they laugh at me and call me names,
They never allow me to play any of their games.

My heart is hurt,
By the people that always blurt.

I had a dream,
That life had seemed,
Too good to be true,
As I found a friend just like you.

Emma Clarke (15)
Farnborough School Technology College, Clifton

I Have A Dream

I don't know what the dream is yet,
But one is not to get in debt,
I want to be like John Terry but there's a long way to go,
But if I want to fulfil my dream I've got a lot to show,
We all have an idol or maybe a hero,
But when we all grow up no one wants to be a zero,
We all want to be in fashion with contemporary clothes,
But as we get older nobody knows,
What we will grow up to be,
But we all have an image we want to see,
We all have a career way we want to go,
But until we grow up we won't know,
At the end of this I hope you see,
If you put your mind to it you can be whatever you want to be.

Jamie Birch (15)
Farnborough School Technology College, Clifton

I Have A Dream

I have a dream
That everyone will be at peace
I have a dream
That there will be no more wars
I have a dream
That everyone will be treated equally
I have a dream
That everyone will understand the meaning of life
I have a dream
That everyone will love and cherish life
I have a dream
That my dream will come true
I have a dream.

Thomas Wheadon (14)
Farnborough School Technology College, Clifton

Young Writers - I Have A Dream Reality Bites!

Poem

As I sit and wonder why,
The days and nights just pass me by,
I'm in a world all of my own,
And I have no place to call my home.

I wonder why I'm in this state,
Is it because I'm so full of hate,
All I do is worry and despair,
I would love to breathe fresh new air.

I need a friend to help me with my troubles,
Not the ones that burst my bubbles,
Life is horrible when I'm alone,
Nobody on the other side of the phone.

I want a friend to share my days,
And be able to see the sunshine raise,
No more cloudy days for me,
If I find this friend then I'll be free.

As I walk along the seashore,
I hear the waves roar more and more,
Crashing against the rocks below,
I still feel very, very low.

I decide to end my life when a person stopped me,
Who later in my life became my wife,
All my fears are fading away,
My darkness now becomes a bright new day.

She is my eyes so I can see,
All the beautiful things that surround me,
No more depressing days for me,
Now that my wife's eyes are leading me.

Nikita Adkin (15)
Farnborough School Technology College, Clifton

Winning The Hardest Race Of All

'Help! Help!' I heard someone cry out,
All I could hear was a scream and a shout,
A huge crowd all surrounding together,
As I walked past, I just thought, *oh whatever,*
But then a helicopter arrived,
I looked down very surprised,
There in the water was a young boy,
The water was tossing him around like a toy,
But then it was too late,
The boy went down like water through a grate,
Nobody was helping, the helicopter stood still,
I thought I would have to save him on my bill,
I ran down the banks and jumped in the water,
But wait, what if he was dead? That would be torture,
However I knew what I had to do and I did it.
I pierced through the water with him on my belly,
He was all floppy like a piece of jelly,
I swam to the side and laid him on the grass,
He then took a breath and all my fear had passed,
I had just won the hardest race of all,
The race against time to save someone's life.

Kayleigh Desnos (13)
Farnborough School Technology College, Clifton

Dear Nottingham . . .

Dear Nottingham, there's battles on the streets,
Everywhere you go innocent people getting beat,
And every time you move it's like blisters on your feet,
This is an example of society's defeat.

Dear Nottingham, gun crime is getting worse,
There are too many kids taken away in a hearse,
This place needs to be tipped and reversed,
This world is like another Egyptian mummy curse.

Dear Nottingham, theft is gonna harm,
You wake up in the morning to a bunch of car alarms,
This place is getting worse, like dying cattle on a farm.

Dear Nottingham, we need to stay together as one,
If we don't, you know that Nottingham is gone?
We've been an alright society but that was not for long,
That's because we let ourselves slip and that's just wrong.

Dear Nottingham, we could fight like soldiers,
To keep this society lightly on our shoulders,
But until then we will be rolling like boulders,
Nothing will happen till we act older . . .

Robert Parnham (14)
Farnborough School Technology College, Clifton

My Life

When I was younger my life was a mess
All that beating and hurting, no wonder I was stressed
I used to love school, never wanted to go home
When the home time bell went, I used to bawl
Stepped through that blue door
Straight up the creaky stairs, shaking like a leaf
As the footsteps came to me like big bears,
His big spotty head, and Harry Potter glasses,
Screamed at me as I sat on my shabby bed,
I did nothing more than obey this monster,
As it was easier that way than ending up as a helpless little ant
                                              screaming for help
Plus, I never knew what he was capable of doing next,
I'd run downstairs as fast as I could, but sometimes I was not
                                              fast enough.

When Mum went out I used to hope and pray,
That someday all this abuse would just fly away,
I mean a little girl shouldn't go through this distress,
All that beating and hurting, no wonder my life was a mess,
He was my brother I didn't know anymore,
I thought all brothers had done this before,
He stripped my nerves right down to the core,

But then there was hope, a ray of light, that little angel came into sight,
They fought and forced for me to be safe, it just goes to show what
                                              families will do.

Your life is supposed to begin the day you are born,
But until I was 8 mine was taken away and torn,
You see that's when my life began, when I was eight
After that I was no longer bait,
It took a little longer I know and you'll see,
How glorious my life is and how happy I can be.

So you see, I know when I was younger my life was a mess,
All that beating and hurting, and all that stress,
But all that stuff has gone out the window,
Well, maybe the stress remains, like a tree left in a meadow.

Erin Bower (14)
Farnborough School Technology College, Clifton

I Have A Dream

If a Year 11 stopped a frail Year 7, and attacked her
and stole her purse,
The fact that others are advised 'not to get involved', would only
make it worse,
Even though it's possible they'd never forget the frightful day,
They'd bow their heads against the rain and hurry on their way.

I have a dream that everyone should recognise love's worth,
That war and conflict would halt, everywhere on Planet Earth,
And that everyone on this world should teach and show respect,
Regardless of disability, gender or any birth defect.

I sit down in school and I brandish a writing pen,
Got inspired to write this poem, for I was teased again
Makes me so angry that others think it's amusing to hurt another,
Be it classmate, cousin, passer-by, or their younger brother.

And I have a dream that seems so big, it makes me give a smile,
When I meet some truly devoted kids who'd honestly run a mile,
To help their friends and family, it makes me think, 'it would . . .
. . . Be great if everyone cared so much as you!
It'd do the world an awful lot of good!'

I know there's a special priceless gift that Heaven above sends,
It's called love - shown in the faces of your family and friends,
The world may be unfriendly and nasty, so it would seem
And it would be so much better with a little more love,
Which is why I have this dream.

Elizabeth Murray (15)
Hagley Park Sports College, Rugeley

I Have A Dream

I have a dream
I have a dream that is fantastic
I have a dream where all my wishes come true
I have a dream that I wish would come true

In my dream wishes come true
In my dream I am pretty and safe
In my dream I have a family
In my dream we are all happy

My dream takes place somewhere special
My dream is set in a world where no wars take place
My dream is in a world where there is no global warming,
My dream is the ideal world we all wish we had.

The dream I have is spectacular,
The dream I have is something I really want,
The dream I have, you'd want it to happen too,
The dream I have is sadly impossible.

I have a dream
I have a dream that is fantastic,
I have a dream where all my wishes come true,
I have a dream that I wish would come true.

Amber Harrison (15)
Hagley Park Sports College, Rugeley

To Make The World A Better Place

I have a dream
About making the world a better place

I have a dream
That there is no terrorism in the world,
And that everybody feels safe,
To make the world a better place.

I have a dream,
That everybody gets along,
And each others relationships become strong,
To make the world a better place.

I have a dream
That other natural resources are found fast,
To replace the old oil, coal and gas
To make the world a better place.

I have a dream
About making the world a better place.

Robert Murdoch (15)
Hagley Park Sports College, Rugeley

I Have A Dream Of Fat Cats

I have a dream that politics will be abolished
The fat cats of parliament will miaow and call no more
Their lies and deceit feathering their own nests as only
                                    buzzards could do
They leave the pickings for the nation
Do they have waiting lists?
Do they have a dentist?
Do they drive huge, gas guzzling cars?
Of course they do.
Wouldn't you?

Ashley Draper (13)
St James' School, Grimsby

I Have A Dream

I have a dream
No screams in this dream
No murder for money
But everything as sweet as honey.

I have a dream
Everyone part of the team,
Where the grass is green,
Nobody mean.

I have a dream,
No drugs and crying shame,
This isn't a game,
Nobody with a false name.

I have a dream,
Where there is no first team,
Everyone to be free, finding love
Everything as peaceful as the dove.

I have a dream,
No theme in this dream,
No addicts,
No one contradicts.

I have a dream,
No screams in this dream,
No murder for money,
Everything sweet as honey.

Daisy Jones (13)
St James' School, Grimsby

I Have A Dream

I have a dream,
Like a fast flowing stream,
Of thoughts and fantasies.
A place to hide,
Dry the tears I've cried,
A refugee from the world outside.
I dream of fairy tales, dragons in flight,
Castles bathed in pale moonlight.
Far off places, swirling seas,
Princesses and mysteries.
Happiness, romance
True love at first glance.
A world of peace,
Wars will cease,
Harmony between nations.
I'm lost in a land of dreams,
I wake and all I hear are screams.
Screams of the poor, sick and dying,
A desperate baby's lonely crying.
Silent tears reflecting pain,
Everyone's loss, no one's gain.
I have a dream,
Like a fast flowing stream,
Of hopes and fantasies.
It sweeps me along,
To where I belong . . .
My perfect land of dreams.

Alice Twomey (13)
St James' School, Grimsby

Life Will Change

I have a dream
That life will be fair
No one will be treated differently
Either for skin colour, race or religion

I have a dream
That pain and suffering will end,
Care will be given,
And war will never start nor end.

I have a dream,
Cancer will be cured,
Life expectancy will increase,
And people will be fitter.

I have a dream,
Of marriage and
To have children
And later grandchildren.

I have a dream
To die and rise to Heaven,
That I will meet God
Find my sins repented.

Sarah Browne (15)
St James' School, Grimsby

Horses Have Dreams

I have a dream that all horses
Can run and jump the greatest courses
To neigh - not run away
From the vandals and hooligans who prey,
Upon us innocent creatures!
To dream of long green grass of meadows and
Sweet smelling hay.

Not to pull carts and survive each day.

Holly Tumber (13)
St James' School, Grimsby

I Have A Dream

I have a dream
That everyone will help each other and
There won't be any war
I have a dream
That everyone is special,
I have a dream,
That there are no enemies,
I have a dream,
That everyone is beautiful,
I have a dream,
That most things are free,
I have a dream,
That everyone is rich,
I have a dream,
That everyone is perfect,
I have a dream,
That no one ruled the world,
I have a dream,
That I am a dancing queen,
I have a dream,
That one day I will have a mansion,
I have a dream,
That there is good health,
I have a dream,
That cats live forever,
I have a dream,
That books rule over computers,
I have a dream,
That will last forever,
So, that's my dream.

Rebecca Procter (12)
St James' School, Grimsby

I Have A Dream

I have a dream that fears isn't real,
That life's a fair deal.
To make people know the meaning of love,
Tell your love you love them send a message by dove.

Show the world that dreams come true,
Dreams can come true though it takes time to do,
Oh dear people of the world think of those who suffer.
Oh poor children with no brothers, sisters or mothers.

Thank the Lord for the deep blue waters and the drifting tides,
Oh the beauty when the sea glides,
Travel the world and the seven seas,
When you've seen the poverty and the glory come and tell me,

Think of people stuck in the shadows desperate to see the shining sun.
Think of people stuck where the sun beams down hard,
But what can be done?

Believe me my darlings, it aches me to see young hearts disappointed,
Full of misery.
Well I've told you my dream,
I hope it will help solve the sadness and misery of all the world.

Lucy Smith (13)
St James' School, Grimsby

I Have A Dream

I have a dream
That people can dream whatever they want to dream
Let them see and hear what they want to
Let them conquer and succeed in what they choose
And most of all don't stop them from being them.

I am living the dream,
That people are cruel and tormenting,
Treating people rough because they have something different
                                          and unique,
Most of these people could never live up to these things.

Anon
St James' School, Grimsby

Dreams

I have a dream, when I go to sleep
That the next day when I wake up there will be,
Harmony and peace in the world,
There shall be no greed,
No selfishness,
No evil, no war,
No bombings, and killings causing death.
Instead the world to be full of love,
To be full of happiness,
To be full of joyfulness,
I wish everyone to be pleased with themselves,
And bring joy to others,
Everyone should have someone to care for and someone to care
                                                                for them,

Someone to love and someone to love them,
We should all be given courage,
And kindness,
We all have these gifts even if we can't see it,
They are there, maybe very deep down,
You'll find them some day,
But this dream may not come true yet, but maybe one day!
At least not today, not today
We shall always hope,
Keep hoping,
Until one day it's not just a dream,
I have a dream that some day my dream shall come true!

Amelia Carroll (12)
St James' School, Grimsby

I Have A Dream

I have a dream to stop all the hurt,
To stop all the pain,
To make the world alert,
I want to be a superwoman,
And spread my joy,
I want to shout out loud,
And not be coy,
I want love to be expressed,
Not hidden away,
Tell everyone . . .
Because you only have one true love,
That's what they say,
No one is different,
We are all the same,
No matter the colour of our skin,
No matter our name,
We should not say who can come into 'our' country,
We should all live together,
As God said we should,
Forever and ever . . .

I have a dream, that my dream comes true!

Mia Champion (14)
St James' School, Grimsby

I Have A Dream About Cruelty

I have a dream that the world would have no war,
People are nice instead of acting like lice,
People should appreciate what God put before us,
And the government are ruining it for us.
I think all the war should stop for God's sake,
Every night a kid who is scared will shake,
So I've got a message for y'all who don't believe,
In war our only weapon is our refusal.

Brian McCarthy (13)
St James' School, Grimsby

I Have A Dream . . . The Importance Of Learning!

I have a dream to see the world
And help those people in need,
Because I think that's the right thing to do.
I would like to help a crowd,
That would appreciate my help,
And learn from things I have taught them,
Most importantly I would like
The rest of the world to appreciate me!

I have a dream for those I help they would,
Then in turn help others,
And to teach others that helping is a good thing,
Also learning from others is also important.
Most of all I dream everyone should respect
Each other regardless of race, creed or colour!

Oliver Woods (12)
St James' School, Grimsby

A Preposterous Dream

I have a dream that I want to be a football player
I have a dream that I can fly in the sky
I have a dream that I have lots of money
I have a dream that I can breathe in the water
I have a dream that I have all the friends I need
I have a dream that I can do what I want
I have a dream that I will not die
I have a dream of everything
I have a dream that I will be the ball
That scores the goal
The greatest of all
My dream will be
To be kicked at Wembley
My dream will come true
When I am kicked by Rooney's shoe!

Nicolas Kong (13)
St James' School, Grimsby

I Have A Dream

I have a dream
Of a perfect world
A world without the mean
A world in which we will be free
In which peace and love can be seen

I have a dream
That we will live forever
In perfect harmony
Where there will be no war
Or issues with things like money

I have a dream
Of no racism
In all of the sports teams
Where there is no cheating, or fixing results
And all is as it seems.

Damon Williams (12)
St James' School, Grimsby

My Perfect World

I have a dream,
That candy will fall from the heavens,
I have a dream,
Of a free world,
I have a dream,
That all wars will end,
I have a dream,
That I will rule the Earth,
And my henchman will be Smurfs,
I have a dream,
For everybody to be rich,
I have a dream,
For a peaceful planet,
I have a dream!

Dean Parkinson (12)
St James' School, Grimsby

My Dream

I have a dream of fluffy, pink candyfloss
Instead of funky, green, wet moss
Where there are no sugar-craving 8-year-olds
Who are energetic and their teeth are made of mould
Where I am president of the world
And all the candy canes have been curled
Where all the people are curled up at my feet
Because I am oh so sweet
But first I'll give 200 grand
To the world's most poorest land.

Charles Sears (12)
St James' School, Grimsby

I Have A Dream

I have a dream
To live life to the full
To live till I'm 100

I have a dream
To travel the world
To see the seven wonders

I have a dream
To be successful
In what I want to do

I have a dream
To fall in love
To have a fairy-tale ending

I have a dream
To help the human race
For people to see there's more beyond a face

I have a dream to be curious.

Georgia Pengelley (11)
St Sampson's Secondary School, St Sampson's

I Have A Dream

My dream is a simple dream to wave
A flag seam by seam
And defend the nation
From humiliation

Yes my dream is a hard-to-get goal
To help the nation with my soul
To find a way to help us all
Until I can hardly crawl

Yes my dream is a long-seen shot
To destroy poverty, yes the whole lot
And wipe out crime
Like cleaning up grime

My dream is a simple sight
To make a stand or even a fight
To kill the threatening notes to us lot
And put the evil in a pot

My dream is a thing
It can't be accomplished with a slight ping
World peace is what I'm hoping for
I don't think you can wish for more.

David Wickham (12)
St Sampson's Secondary School, St Sampson's

I Have A Dream

I have a dream,
To be a pilot,
Soar in the skies,
Of peace and harmony,
See the beauty of
A free world.

I have a dream,
Everyone will be friends,
No person will be judged,
By how they look or
Who they are.

I have a dream,
To prove it is what is on
The inside of a person
Not the outside.

I have a dream,
That we will all be free,
All countries are best friends,
No hate in the world.

I have a dream,
That the birds of peace,
Harmony and freedom,
Soar the sky in the morning sun.

Daniel Ridley (11)
St Sampson's Secondary School, St Sampson's

My Dream

I don't know what lies ahead
But I have one dream
A dream that there will be peace
For me and for you.

I want a world that is free from war,
And I want to see you when I open the door,
I just want a world that is free from war.

Everything's too modern,
Everything's too new,
I just want peace,
For me and for you.

I can't believe what's happening, the world is free from war,
I saw you when I opened the door,
I've got a world that is free from war.

My dream of peace,
My dream of you,
Has definitely come true.

Leanne Oliver (11)
St Sampson's Secondary School, St Sampson's

I Have A Dream

To be able to complete a game,
That is my dream,
You may think that's lame,
But that's what I call mean.

I turn on my PlayStation every day
To think what am I to do,
There is no other way,
Other than thinking it through.

That is my dream,
Still not complete,
But I hope that by tomorrow,
It will be crawling at my feet.

Daniel De Carteret (11)
St Sampson's Secondary School, St Sampson's

Imagine It

Imagine
No hatred in the world
Imagine
A world with love, kindness and laughter
Imagine,
Two races coming together and joining as one,
Imagine,
A fresh start to a day,
Imagine,
A world which is filled with happiness,
Imagine,
Unity,
Imagine,
A healthy new life,
Imagine,
Strength in all our dreams and wishes,
Imagine,
No need to use our imagination and making our imagination today.

Bethany De La Mare (11)
St Sampson's Secondary School, St Sampson's

I Have A Dream

I have a dream that I will . . .
Be a super model and be on the cover of a magazine.
I have a dream that I will . . .
Score my best shot in a netball match and be the best.
I have a dream that I will . . .
Stop all wars and poverty, give everyone freedom
I have a dream that I will . . .
Become a successful business woman,
And be able to give people what they want.
I have a dream that no one has . . .
Which is that we can have happiness
For me and for you!

Natalie Miranda (12)
St Sampson's Secondary School, St Sampson's

The World Was A Better Place

One day my dream will come true,
My dream was that the world was a better place.

In my dream there were no more thugs and no
More drugs and the world was a nice place.

There were no more punks and no more drunks
And the world was a better place.

Martin Luther King once mentioned
Something about black and white,
That they should reunite
Because in my dream racism was stamped out
And you could see black and white friends walking about.

In my dream there was no more pleading and everybody was healing
The poor and misfortunate,
So as my dream came to an end,
All I could do was think and wonder what the world could be like.

Will Garnett (12)
St Sampson's Secondary School, St Sampson's

I Have A Dream

I have a dream of being in a football team
I want to play in the championship
Perhaps one day I will play in the Premiership
Playing next to Robbie Keane
That will be the weirdest thing I have ever seen
I have a dream of being in a football team
Before I go on the pitch I hear the crowd say my name,
That's why I love the game,
I have a dream of being in a football team,
I have a dream of being seen, on the TV screen,
I wish I could score a goal,
Just like Andy Cole,
I have a dream of being in a football team.

Marcus Heaume (12)
St Sampson's Secondary School, St Sampson's

I Have A Dream

I have a dream that one day there will be peace,
No war and no fights,
Everyone will get along,
And in years to come everyone's criminal record will be blank.

I have a dream everyone is who they are,
And it won't matter what skin colour you are,
I believe bullying can and will be stamped out,
You just wait and watch.

I have a dream that everything about you will stay that way,
And your hobbies and interests will stay different from your peers,
I hope and pray that maybe some day,
Everyone will know where they stand and know their own life directions.

I have a dream that some day everyone respects others
As if they were friends,
And aren't afraid of anyone else,
I have a dream . . .
Dream . . .
Dream . . .
Dream . . .
I have a dream!

Rachel Tulie (11)
St Sampson's Secondary School, St Sampson's

I Have A Dream

I have a dream to be rich
I have a dream to be famous
I also have a dream to stamp out poverty,
Racism and terrorism.
I have a dream to live forever,
To make sure everyone else does too
Those are some of my dreams,
What are yours?

Donna Gallienne (12)
St Sampson's Secondary School, St Sampson's

The Future By A 12-Year-Old Schoolboy

Classroom stress deadlines to keep,
It's enough to make a schoolboy weep,
Algebra, French and RE,
Homework to do all before tea.

When I get older no more school,
Have to play by a different set of rules,
Work very hard give plenty of devotion,
This is what's needed to get a promotion.

Shall play lots of hockey be in a team,
Try to get noticed want to be seen,
Maybe someday I'll have a wife,
This is a great view of my life.

Adrian Lancaster (12)
St Sampson's Secondary School, St Sampson's

My Dream

I have a dream
That my family and me have a happy life
I have a dream
That when I'm older I can live my life the way I dream of living it
I have a dream
That one day I can have a family of my own
I have a dream
That my brother and sister can do what they want in the future
I have a dream
That people can act and be treated exactly the same as other people
I have a dream
That there is no fear or violence in the world
Those are my dreams.

Elise De La Mare (12)
St Sampson's Secondary School, St Sampson's

I Have A Dream

The lives that are lost,
The blood that is spread,
The savages that are on this Earth,
The brutal men,
The selfish hearts are all that rules the Earth,
Unjust, cold-blooded, cruelty and brutality
This is all that rules the Earth.
Blood drips down their faces,
Unhappiness rules the Earth.

Tranquillity and serenity is what this world should be,
The calmness and the quietness is what this world should be,
Peace and quiet, laughter and friends, love and smiles
Should make the world go round.
Level-headedness and coolness is all the world should be . . .

Which world do you want to live in?

Jennie Wheeler (13)
Swanmore Middle School, Ryde

Drought

Drought is bad
It will make people sad
It's happening in England
That's why there's a hosepipe ban

The water is low
Sometimes water will go
If the ground is hard and you scrape your toe
You'll fall on the ground and go, 'Oh, oh, oh!'

Africa is the place where the drought is being held,
It is killing loads of people every year in the world,
The kids and the adults,
Try to survive in the world.

The Africans pray,
'For the rain to come!'

Harry Brown (12)
Swanmore Middle School, Ryde

Bullying

Every day I go to school,
Everywhere I go I hear them call,
When I'm listening to the teacher I hear threats,
'I'm going to beat you.'
After lesson they are there,
They grab me from the back of my hair,
I scream and shout, 'Leave me be,'
But then they kick me in the knee.
They call me names I cannot repeat,
Then my heart skips a beat,
My mind stops and I am thinking,
What have I done to deserve this beating?

Bullying is wrong
It's not right!
Some people cry
All day and night!

Kara Gregory (13)
Swanmore Middle School, Ryde

I Had A Dream

I had a dream
About great Africa
I saw all the horrors
And all the suffering
The poor African people have to endure,
Why do the children have nothing to eat?
Not a scrap of vegetable or meat,
Why do the children have little clothes?
Maybe because people think they're foes,
Why do the children not have enough water?
Why do the parents have to suffer from the death of a son or daughter?
Why do the rich countries have no care?
I just don't see how that is fair
So if you have some money spare
Please could you share?

Dennis Kurtin (11)
Swanmore Middle School, Ryde

I Have A Dream

She wakes up in the morning
Examines her face
The one that's going to get her through another day,
It doesn't really matter,
How she feels inside,
As life gets her down sometimes.

Smashing and crashing, falling through her mind,
She wonders if her father's kind
Heaving herself up, feeling cold,
She feels as it her life's been sold,
Shouting echoing through the house,
She sits there shaking - quiet as a mouse,
Rocking herself to and fro,
Will she be here tomorrow?
She doesn't know.

Running down the stairs, out the door,
With blood trickling down to the floor,
She does this to herself as she cannot cope,
All she can do in her mind is hope.

Come home from school to find a list of chores on the table,
She has to do these to make her life stable,
If life has doors then she's locked out,
She doesn't fit in, can't even shout out,
All she wants is to feel loved,
To feel special, this would be the perfect life for her,
This is what her life's like Sir.

Louisa Johns (13)
Swanmore Middle School, Ryde

Bullying

See how they push him
Push him around
See how they kick him
Kick him to the ground
I stand there in horror
As they stomp on his face
All those who did it
Scurry away.

The voice of the teachers,
The yells, screams and shouts.
All seems so distant,
As if a mile out.

But I notice none of this,
As a life drips away.
Drips from my fingers,
Not to see another day.

Why do we bully
If we know it hurts so?

Tommy Andrews (13)
Swanmore Middle School, Ryde

I Have A Dream

I had a dream
With no gleam
People dying
People crying
Young children in a very bad mood,
People with a non-stop craving for food,
The sky is black on a warm summer's day,
With pollution taking the ozone layer away
Some little kids have no dad,
While pollution is killing like mad.

Jake Mummery (12)
Swanmore Middle School, Ryde

Child Abuse

She was small and dainty,
Upset and fainty,
She searched and searched for food and drink,
No time at all to stop and think,
Screaming and shouting,
Dad is belting,
Mum takes it out on her.

New day, new tears
More stress, more beers
To all of them pain is so near,
This is awful, all of the fear,
The baby is in agony, starving and upset,
Poor baby's life is at threat,
Hospital trips are endless.

Mum finally realises what she has done,
Now baby doesn't run,
She throws out Dad,
He didn't care, not even a tad,
Now Mum and baby are on the mend,
It's like baby has a new best friend,
The next few years are up to Mum.

The baby is now nine,
Mum and daughter get on just fine,
Apart from tiny little squabbles,
About little bobbles,
They both live a fantastic life,
Baby's life was turned into the light,
I'm surprised she is still alive.

Amy Smith (13)
Swanmore Middle School, Ryde

War

Why, why do we have war?
Make children's eyes all salty and sore?
Spread anger and hatred all over the land,
When children should sing, hand in hand

How can people kill each other?
Every child without a mother
All alone without a dad,
Or a husband, it's very sad.

I saw a man, standing alone
Broken, hurt and away from home,
He stood on the corner, covered in blood
My eyes filled up as if they would flood.

So ask yourself this, why should we fight
Keeping children awake and frightened at night?
Why do we hate and kill each other,
When we should stand together, like sister and brother?

Rosie Barrett (13)
Swanmore Middle School, Ryde

I Have A Dream

The way they always stop and stare
The way they always pull my hair,
The way they give me dirty looks
The way they always steal my books.

When they start to scream and shout,
When they start to push me about,
When they start to say I'm insane,
And make it out like I'm not the same.

What they're doing they just don't see
That what they are doing is hurting me,
What they do to get attention,
Ends up putting me in detention.

Now listen up all you out there,
Who just don't seem to even care,
Stop and think before you act,
And the world would be better and that's a fact.

Michelle Turpin (13)
Swanmore Middle School, Ryde

I Have A Dream

The perfect world . . .

No need . . .

For exercise
To run
To be afraid
For medicine
For being ill
For drugs
For alcohol
For racism.

Our world is perfect
No need for sadness,
We have equal money,
We are united,
We have different qualities,
We all have experience,
We all like different things,
We are perfect . . .

Oliver Ryan (13)
Swanmore Middle School, Ryde

War

My dream is no war!

War is all around us
War is on the ground around us
War is cruel
People think it's cool

War contains killing
And it's not very thrilling
War is bloody
War is pretty muddy

War is frightening
War is scary
Families get split up
Or maybe worse, evacuated.

War, why do people have to suffer?
Why is war a threat?
War is nasty
So my dream is to forget.

Archie Sampson (12)
Swanmore Middle School, Ryde

My Dream Is This

I have a dream,
Though small I seem,
In time this world will follow.

For if they don't,
Survive they would,
And in sorrow they will wallow.

As Earth goes down the pan,
We couldn't give a damn,
Sleeping snugly in our beds,
Why can't we use our heads?

With cars we choke our planet,
With ice we try to fan it,
But cars would win a war,
Of that I can be sure.

You must want to help now,
And to do this you must use,
Recycled wood and plastic,
Chairs, tables and shoes.

Another way to help Earth,
To save our troubled land,
Is to publicise our cause,
Come and give us a hand.

Nico Burns (13)
Swanmore Middle School, Ryde

Continent Disaster

Africa, Tanzania, poverty
Famine, hunger, poor and deprived
They don't deserve it, they should be free!

Asia, Iraq, war
Conflict, fighting, rivalry
A ghostly alliance existing no more.

Australasia, New Zealand, suicide
Misery, pain and suffering
No one to run to, nowhere to hide.

Europe, England, abuse
Assault, ill treatment, harm
These vile people still on the loose.

Antarctica, South Pole, global warming
Climate change, heating up
We all know that trouble is forming.

North America, USA, racism
Bigotry, discrimination, hatred
'Cause of other people's terrorism.

South America, Brazil, pollution
Contamination, poison
Is this 'greener' Earth's contribution?

Problems? Yes.
Solutions? Yes.

Eloise de Carvalho (12)
Swanmore Middle School, Ryde

Dehydration

People dying
Children crying
Dehydration
Kills a nation.

Parched cattle,
Fight a battle,
Against the heat,
So they can eat.

A newborn baby,
Who's dying maybe,
Cries for Mum,
But she's already gone.

People dying,
Children crying,
Dehydration,
Kills a nation.

Grace Hannington (12)
Swanmore Middle School, Ryde

HIV

HIV is a horrible disease
A disease which lets germs in with ease
HIV is a big killer
If you had it you'd think it wasn't a thriller
HIV has no cure,
If you've had it you won't want more,
I think you'd do anything, not to get that awful thing
If you got it you would cry and cry and cry until you die,
I had a dream that the disease was cured.

Tom Taylor (11)
Swanmore Middle School, Ryde

Why?

Why? Why?
I really tried,
They just lied,
And made me cry,
I felt alone,
I wanted to go home,
I hurt inside,
I wished I had died,
But now I have told someone,
That person is my mum,
She helped me pull through,
So now I have no fear,
Knowing my mum will always be here,
I know she will support me,
Through good times and bad,
So thank you Mum,
And you too Dad.

Reegan Greenwood (11)
Swanmore Middle School, Ryde

Homeless Him

No one cares
Why is he there?
Sat outside the shops
Looking out for any cops
People give him dirty looks
They also give him names like 'crook'
All the kids laugh
When they walk past
It's not fair
He shouldn't be there
But what else can he do?
That's what I'm asking you.

Kym Tims (12)
Swanmore Middle School, Ryde

Smoking

Smoking is serious
You should stop soon
It turns your lungs black
Like a cloud covered moon
It gives you bad breath
With the putrid smoke
You find breathing hard
The tar makes you choke
It stains all your clothes
As well as your teeth
Really good health
The thing smoking loathes
Smoking's your foe
It's very unhealthy
So always remember
To smoking say no.

Joe Peduzzi (12)
Swanmore Middle School, Ryde

Poverty

Miles to water,
Not educated,
Hungry every day,
And dehydrated.

In old clothes,
Babies dying,
Children on streets,
Orphans crying.

Bad nutrition,
Children ill,
AIDS killing,
How would you feel?

Mollie Valvona (12)
Swanmore Middle School, Ryde

Watching Or Helping?

Watching people lying there,
Coughing, choking, dying there.
How can you just sit there that's not polite?
I can't even manage to sleep at night.
Knowing that little kids have lost their mums,
Scared in corner sucking their thumbs.
What is this world coming to?
I think it should be made anew,
This world where HIV/AIDS are around,
People doing nothing sitting on the ground.

Watching these kids on a bed of death,
With everything gone and nothing left,
We always have events to make them money,
How come it's never enough for bread and honey?
Thousands of children die each day,
For the one reason they don' t get enough pay,
You may think these problems will go away,
But they never will with HIV/AIDS,
I think we can stop all this I really do,
But it will never go unless you help too.

Cassandra Loe (12)
Swanmore Middle School, Ryde

Racism

They constantly call me names,
But somehow I get the blame.

They viciously kick my stuff,
I wish I was more tough.

But one day it went too far,
I can still see that speeding car.

I can still feel that sudden pain,
Like the stinging whip of a cane.

I hope they're locked behind bars,
Whilst I'm sleeping amongst the stars.

I know they will have to pay,
When comes their judgement day.

Just because the colour of my skin,
We're all the same within . . .

Emma Beak (12)
Swanmore Middle School, Ryde

We All Have Dreams!

I have a dream that there is no
More pollution in the air
I have a dream that there is
No more bullying or despair
I have a dream that wars and arguments
Are no more
I have a dream of no more
Children getting hurt
I have a dream that this is
What we all deserve.

Laura Stevens (13)
The Channel School, Folkestone

I Have A Dream

I have a dream that
There will be no more animal cruelty
The animals don't deserve it.

I have a dream that
Everyone will believe in themselves,
Do everything they want to do.

I have a dream that,
That there will be no more wars or bullying.

I have a dream that,
When I'm older I will get a job working with old people.
I have a dream that
I will get the GCSEs that I want,
Which will help me get a good job.

My biggest wish is that my dream will come true.

Karianne Jewkes (12)
The Channel School, Folkestone

I Have A Dream

I have a dream of a wonderful world
Where no wars or violence occur
No nasty drugs, crime or homelessness
No bullies in my world.
My mum, dad and family live forever,
I dream of a lovely life,
Plenty of money to do all the things that make me happy,
I dream I will meet Richard Fleeshman!
I dream he will fall in love with me and live happily ever after,
I dream I will be a big star like him,
I dream my dream will come true!

Danielle Gough (14)
The Channel School, Folkestone

I Have A Dream

I have a dream that bullies don't exist and everyone gets on, no
fighting
I have a dream that people all round the world will have enough food
and water
So that nobody dies of thirst
I have a dream that parents will not abuse their children and
Children don't abuse their parents
I have a dream that racism will stop
Black people will not abuse white people
And white people will not abuse black people.
I have a dream that when you go out at night
You will not be afraid to be out on the streets because of killings
and rapists
I have a dream that the criminals on the street will stop stealing and
doing bad things
I have a dream for a world without war and for everyone to get on
I have a dream that people do not throw litter on the floor.

Stephanie Cole (12)
The Channel School, Folkestone

I Have A Dream

I have a dream that I will die happy
I have a dream that I will be a hairdresser
I have a dream that I can get the homeless off the streets
I have a dream that all of my friends will be happy when they are older
I have a dream that my brothers and sisters will be happy
I have a dream that crime will all stop
I have a dream that all the people who have cancer will be cured
I have a dream that I can give my soul to everyone to share
my dreams.

Nicola McDonagh (14)
The Channel School, Folkestone

A Perfect World

I have a dream that one day there will be no wars
I have a dream that there will be world peace
I have a dream that black and whites will hold hands
I have a dream that there will be no world hunger
I have a dream that there will be no drought.

I have a dream that there will be medicines and treatment
                                        for all countries.
I have a dream that treatment for cancer will be found
I have a dream that there will be no more crimes
I have a dream that there will be no more criminals

I have a dream for everyone to be kind to each other
                                        and no bullying
I have a dream for people to live in peace
I have a dream for schools and hospitals to have more money
I have a dream that people will be treated the same
I have a dream that everyone will have all the technology

I have a dream to end all dreams.

Christopher Hadlington (13)
The Channel School, Folkestone

I Have A Dream

I have a dream to travel the world
See all the beautiful things in the universe,
I dream of a world with no crime, just honesty,
So everyone lives happy and has a nice life as one,
I dream that there are no bullies and wish everyone were seen
                                        as equal,

I dream that there's no cruelty to animals,
So there is more animal protection,
I dream of a perfect place to grow up in,
That has trees and water for all the countries,
If we all dream this, maybe it will come true.

Megan Hart (14)
The Channel School, Folkestone

I Have A Dream

I have a dream, that our generations can make a change to this world
I have a dream that we can all live as brothers and sisters
Without our religions causing chaos
I have a dream that all people will love and care for others.

My dream is that I can be rich,
But that will not help the others in the world,
I have a dream that religions will forget about conflict and
Live together in harmony as one.

My dream is that one day we can live without racism,
Hatred and poverty amongst us.
I have a dream that war will be no more,
I have a dream, a dream I hope will come true
A dream for me and you.

Francisco Gomes (14)
The Channel School, Folkestone

My Dream

I have a dream that people will change
Our nightmares and fears will go away
I have a dream that people from other countries will not have
                                        any poverty
I know what this feels like.
That's what I call cruelty - not enough to eat or drink.
I have a dream that sadness will magic into happiness because
The Devil is looking for sad souls.
He ruins lives with drugs, coke and LSD, that's the Devil's food.
I dream to keep me going - I rap to keep me safe,
My rap dreams are my safe house,
Dream and be safe.

Sabrijan Juniku (14)
The Channel School, Folkestone

I Have A Dream

I have a dream,
To stop wars,
So that everyone in the world will be friends not enemies,
To stop global warming.

I have a dream,
To do well in school,
To have a good job,
To stop bullying.

I have a dream,
That everyone in the world to be cured of cancer and all illnesses,
All the endangered animals in the world to be saved,
And save all the rainforests that are being cut down.

I have a dream,
For all the homeless people in the world to have homes,
And a loving family,
That everyone will recycle and save the world from
Running out of resources.

I have a dream,
For all the suffering families throughout the world to
Have clean water and fresh food every day.

I have a dream,
That no one will suffer again.

And I hope that the world will become a better place,
So everyone will live in peace for generations to come.

Mikyla Melville (12)
The Channel School, Folkestone

I Have A Dream

I have a dream
The poor will be rich
Everyone has friends
The war ends

I have a dream
Everyone has someone special and is loved
All families are reunited
Black and white are treated the same

I have a dream
That everyone is treated fairly no matter what they look like
Everyone is happy
That maybe I can help someday

I have a dream
That all my dreams happen
That the world had peace
To reach my goals

But my biggest dream is everyone has their own special dream.

Rachael Whittle (13)
The Channel School, Folkestone

I Have A Dream

I have a dream that my grandad gets better
I have a dream that I can help all the poor people
I have a dream that I will be a footballer or a break dancer
I have a dream that Tottenham will win the Premiership
I have a dream that I will get a good education
I have a dream that England will win the World Cup
I have a dream that none of my family will ever die
I have a dream that all the poor sick people get better.

Michael Hunt (12)
The Channel School, Folkestone

I Have A Dream

I have a dream that one day war will be no more
That racism is no more
That poverty is no more

I have a dream that together violence and crime will stop forever
I have a dream that together war and poverty will stop forever
I have a dream that us as brothers will make it stop forever.

I have a dream that one day we will all sit at God's table as equals,
I have a dream that we will live in a society with no racism, no crime,
                                                no poverty

I have a dream.

I have a dream that one day the City of London gang trouble
And knife attacks will be forgotten
And that it will be a distant memory.

I have a dream.

Cade Mortimer (13)
The Channel School, Folkestone

I Have A Dream

I have a dream where people will not kill or be violent or cruel
I have a dream where there's no hate or criminals
I have a dream where all people join hands and like each other
I have a dream where there's no threats to other countries
I have a dream where people don't judge people
For what they wear or look like
I have a dream where young people can go to the cinema
Without any threats.
I have a dream where young kids can go round the shop
Without people bullying or taking stuff off them.
I have a dream where there is no war and no killing.

I have a dream.

Cameron Jackson (12)
The Channel School, Folkestone

My Dreams

I have a dream
To reach my goal,
To earn lots of money,
Deep inside my soul.

I have a dream,
To go to college,
To pass my exams,
And to increase my knowledge.

I have a dream,
For my dream to be fulfilled,
It might take a long time,
But I am strong willed.

I have a dream,
A really big dream,
For the world to be full of peace,
And wars will cease.

I have a dream.

Sian Beer (13)
The Channel School, Folkestone

I Have A Dream

I have a dream to be a spaceman
Travel the world in my rocket
I blast off into space
I see Mars, it is my fantasy place
I land on Mars loudly,
I take my first step,
I look around and I dread that -
Aliens will come!
And take me away,
And I may not come back another day.

Paul Williams (14)
The Channel School, Folkestone

Dreaming Ahead

When I grow up I want to be rich
Not a tramp living in a ditch
I'd love to change a lot of things
To be better than all the kings
Rule the world and just feel free
That's what I would like to be
We get what we are giving
For love of how we're living
Poverty happens a lot
And lots of people are shot
I have a dream
And seeing a blazing beam
Love, peace and strength on Earth,
A shame that it couldn't start from birth,
Wars will continue forever and ever,
I would like a lot of things to stop,
But racism would be at the top,
White people should treat black people fair,
Some people may be different by the colour of their hair,
Little black boys holding a little white girl's hand
You can help by wearing an 'against racism' band.
I have a dream
To make my face light up like gleam
One day there will be love and peace
There will not be any police
Do your share
And give your care.

Ross Williams (13)
The Channel School, Folkestone

I Have A Dream

I have a dream that the world will see world peace
I have a dream that racism will stop and disappear into the mist
I have a dream that wars will stop!
I have a dream that black and white will join together,
I have a dream that people will feel safe on the streets,
I have a dream that people won't get bullied,
I have a dream that people will help the poor,
I have a dream that poverty will stop!

Dominic Deeley (12)
The Channel School, Folkestone

I Have A Dream

I have a dream to rule the world over the stars and moon,
I have a dream that everyone will come together as friends,
So we can make the world a completely different place,
Where dreams can come true.

I have a dream that robot people would come and help us
In all different situations.

Liam Staveley (12)
The Channel School, Folkestone

I Have A Dream

I have a dream that one day all wars will stop
I have a dream that people will be treated as equals
I believe that racism will become a myth
I dream that all wars will be shot down and die
I have a dream that people will not live in poverty
But most of all I have a dream that everyone will be equal.

Elliot Ranford (12)
The Channel School, Folkestone

I Have A Dream

I have a dream that poor little children will not be afraid to walk
on the streets
I have a dream that little children will not be neglected by
uncaring parents
I have a dream that families can have a happy life and not get bullied
I have a dream that children will not be afraid of their parents
I have a dream that children will not be afraid to go to school
I have a dream that everyone will be happy one day
I have a dream that war will be no more.

Hayley Langton
The Channel School, Folkestone

I Have A Dream

I have a dream that boys and girls will go out safe and come back safe
I have a dream that people will not be racist to other people
I have a dream that we should help people on the streets that have
no food or money
I have a dream that I can make people stick together, love each other
and never leave each other.
I have a dream that no more crimes will be committed in the world.

Jess Bunker
The Channel School, Folkestone

I Have A Dream

I have a dream that violence and racism will stop going round
I have a dream that black and white people can get on and stop being
nasty and racist
I have a dream that people will stop calling other people
horrible names
I have a dream that rich people will stop showing their money to
poor people.

Alex Smith (13)
The Channel School, Folkestone

I Have A Dream

I have a dream that people shouldn't be unkind to others
                              and live their lives happily
I have a dream that everybody should be friendly with others
I have a dream that you can go out onto the streets,
                    as long as you like without bullies there
I have a dream that people have the money for anything they need
I have a dream that people can be as strong as they like
I have a dream that people get together
I have a dream that racism never existed.

Scott Wilson (12)
The Channel School, Folkestone

I Have A Dream

I have a dream where nice and bad people can play with each other
I have a dream where people should not be racist
I have a dream where people don't kill anybody at night
I have a dream that we should not see people starve and suffer
I have a dream that Tottenham Hotspur will win the UEFA Cup
I have a dream that there should be no school!

Daniel Cole (12)
The Channel School, Folkestone

I Wish

I wish the world was a better place
I wish that there was such a thing as being truly equal
I wish there was no such thing as money and no such thing as debt
I wish all animals would be treated with respect, including humans
I wish that everyone would care about global warming and
Everyone would help preserve the world.
I wish there would be no wars and no unhappiness or anger,
I wish the world was a better place,
That's what I wish.

Rosie Smith (14)
Thomas Alleynes High School, Uttoxeter

I Have A Dream

Anger, adultery, ageism, aggravation, black,
Betrayal, belief, blood, bomb, bleed
Culture, cruelty, crying, children, crime
Cynical, critical, choke, deception, disgrace
Disappointed, disillusioned, dedication, discrimination, depression
Determination, death, dead, dying, deceased
Explicit, erotic, endless, eternity, exile
Eliminate, exodus, extinction, explosion, earthquake
Famine, fatigue, fear, greed, guilt
Gone, genesis, hurt, hunger, hate
Idolism, infatuation, injustice, jaded, jealous
Kicked, killed, lust, lies, loss
Longing, money, mistreat, Middle East, murder
Negativity, neglect, no one, nothing, nowhere
Originality, obliterate, old, pain, poverty
Pierced, poor, punishment, penetration, perverse
Questions, rape, racism, rage, sadness
Self-harm, shame, suicide, sweat, sin
Sorrow, turmoil, threat, torment, terrified,
Tear, tears, treachery, upset, ugly,
Unlovable, untouchable, undone, unlookable, unkissable,
Unlistenable, undesirable, unhappy, vandal, volcano
Worry, wound, wrong, war, weep
When, what, who, where, why
X-rated, young, yearning, you, zero.

In your life you'll experience
One of the world's problems,
Protect our world, there may
Still be a glint of
Hope.

Alison Averill (14)
Thomas Alleynes High School, Uttoxeter

Why?

To go to war or not to go to war
That is what Blair asked
We gave him our answer
But he didn't listen to that.

Now look where we are,
Fighting for another country,
Does he not care that our soldiers are dying,
No, 'cause he's like that.

We see all this anger on TV
We see all this hate
But do we really know what goes on out there
It all just seems so fake

I hate to watch the news
I hate to see the fights
Why can't it all just stop?
Why can't you see the light?

Stacey Bettney (15)
Thomas Alleynes High School, Uttoxeter

I Have A Problem

Why when the world is so beautiful,
Do people have to break the law?
Why do they have to lie and cheat?
What makes them so special?
Are they as stupid as metal?
What's wrong with being good like the rest of us?

When you start the day
Going out in the morning
Do you really want to kill somebody?
Why do you do it?
Do you think you are tough?
Because we don't think it is good, we think it is evil.

Daniel Ardron (15)
Thomas Alleynes High School, Uttoxeter

I Have A Dream - How It Really Is

I lie awake
And wonder why
Would anyone weep if I should die?
The world goes on with endless time
Without a reason or a rhyme
Am I a player in its game?
I hang my head in desperate shame.

Will no one listen, does no one care?
The world's resources, dangerously rare.
The clouds above send acid rain,
The forests cry with humble pain,
The ocean creeps upon the shore,
The glaciers soon will be no more,
The food is short, the people dying
The children sit among the crying.

On the box the MPs shout
Do they know or care about
The plight of pandas, tigers, whales
Who disappear? Their light goes pale.

The seasons seem to be the same,
No summer sun, no autumn rain
The snow at Christmas has all gone,
The spring and summer seem like one.
Will no one listen to the weak,
The old man's voice, can he not speak?
We do not care who picks on who
So long as we can make it through

The world will die and so will we
Then no one's left to weep for me.

Georgie Nash (15)
Thomas Alleynes High School, Uttoxeter

I Have A Dream

I have a dream to be a footballer's wife
Rubies and diamonds yes,
That's what I want from life.

Football matches and free drink too,
Sounds like heaven doesn't it, to you?
Gorgeous hunks all around,
I'm always having to look at the ground.

Glitzy parties and a fancy gown,
Chauffeur driven around the town,
People staring and looking at me,
It makes me feel like royalty.

I finally awake and realise it's a dream,
So life is now not what it seems,
No glitzy parties or fancy gowns,
No chauffeur driving me around the town.

Sharnie Podmore (13)
Thomas Alleynes High School, Uttoxeter

Untitled

Imagine if the world could change,
In such a simple way,
Prejudice would turn to love,
And racism shunned away.

All suffering and pain would leave,
And hate would turn and go,
War would be an unknown corner,
And nobody would know.

If a bomb would turn to sunshine,
A missile into flowers,
Toxins into sweet perfume,
And cover with loving showers.

Daniel Guymer (14)
Thomas Alleynes High School, Uttoxeter

What If

What if
One day violence was unheard of
What if
One day one day no one was taken for granted
What if
One day people of different cultures could mix,
What if
One day there was no such thing as discrimination,
What if,
One day all the countries came together,
What if,
One day one word could make a difference,
What if
One day a smile could change a life,
What if,
One day appearance didn't matter
What if,
One day you could be yourself without being judged,
What if
One day our world was perfect,
What if,
One day there was light in everyone's lives,
What if,
One day everyone could speak their minds,
What if
One day creativity was appreciated,
What if
One day peace filled all our homes,
What if . . .

Clarissa Johnson (14)
Thomas Alleynes High School, Uttoxeter

Imagine

Just imagine that you had millions of pounds
What would you do with it?
You can do anything you want with it
Just imagine
You could help the poor
Just think of the change
You could change someone's life
What would you do with it?
Just imagine all of the things you could buy
What would you buy?
Think of the good things that could come of it,
Just imagine,
You could buy peace
Would you do this?
You could prevent war
Would you?
Just imagine the good,
Just think of the bad,
Just hope that you can make a difference,
Just know that you can,
Just visualise the impact of your money,
And just learn,
That something good can happen because of you
And your wealth!

Tiffany Leadbetter (14)
Thomas Alleynes High School, Uttoxeter

What Do We Call A Dream?

What do we call a dream?
Is it where pigs can fly?
Or when our Prince Charming rescues us from reality
Or even when we are lucky enough to win the lottery
Should we call these dreams?

Is a dream being a rock star?
Playing our songs in front of a wild crowd,
Sweating on stage,
And fulfilling our craziest ambitions,
Is this a dream?

Maybe a dream is when the whole world unites as one,
And joins together . . . forever
Instead of the separation of religions, race and culture
We become one,
Is this a dream?

Will the day come when pigs can fly?
When humans live forever
When cancer is cured
Or when the sky will fall
Is this a dream?

Or is it when all the wars end,
All the violence stops,
And all the outrage finishes,
This is what we call a dream.

Amy Lowe (14)
Thomas Alleynes High School, Uttoxeter

I Have A Dream

If we all live in the same place
What does it matter about the colour of your face
Who cares if you are fat or thin
Who cares about the colour of your skin
They diss people who have a different style
Which makes some people want to go away for a while
Imagine a world without any colour
Colour makes the world seem a little fuller
What does it matter if you are gay,
People say that they lead others astray,
People kill each other and people are dying,
Children and elderly get hurt, can you hear them crying?
Imagine a world without any war,
People become prejudiced more and more,
The world is a terrible place,
Be true to yourself and it would be great,
If we all live in the same place,
Why do people care about the colour of your face?

Paige Martin (14)
Thomas Alleynes High School, Uttoxeter

Imagine

Imagine a world that's not dependent on fossil fuels
That produces clean, cheap, efficient electricity
Where ice caps don't crumble into the sea,
And tsunami, floods and droughts aren't frequent.

Imagine a world where your rubbish powered the country
And the rest was recycled
Where schools produced electricity from light and wind
Where people aren't frightened they'll die because of the electricity
                                                    they're using

Imagine a world where people don't waste electricity
Where objects don't waste energy
Where cars don't pollute the environment
Stop imagining and make it happen!

Jonathan Nash (13)
Thomas Alleynes High School, Uttoxeter

If You Have A Dream

Imagine if you change the world
In one simple day
Make such a difference
In one ordinary day.

So many people have dreamt it,
Save the world, make world peace, do it now
It could be you or anyone,
But only you know how.

But one thing that you really need,
Is courage to shout it out
To say, 'I have a dream'
And say it with no doubt.

So come on you can do it,
We need you to make it through,
We need you, yes you, yes everyone
With you there is nothing we cannot do!

Anna Holdcroft (14)
Thomas Alleynes High School, Uttoxeter

I Have A Dream

Imagine a world without any war
No need for unnecessary death
Imagine a world without any war
Everyone living in peace
Think of a time without any war
No one above all the rest
Think of a time without any war
Without pain or suffering or hurt
Dream of a place without any war
No conflict with good cause
Dream of a place without any war
Countries just getting along
I have a dream that there isn't any war,
I will believe it forever - is that wrong?

Kirsty Pearson (14)
Thomas Alleynes High School, Uttoxeter

Imagine

Imagine
That you could be anything you wanted
Think
Of a world with no fear
Create
A feeling of pride
Win
Any contest you enter
Change
Anything that you hate about yourself
Produce
Eternal life
Dream
What your child will be like
Feel
The luck of the Irish all the time
Destroy
All your problems and troubles
Plan
The way your life will go
Make
The perfect partner
Design
Your perfect house
Have
The perfect job
But would it really be worth it?
Taking away
All that makes life
Interesting?

Holly Dunn (14)
Thomas Alleynes High School, Uttoxeter

Dreams

Dreams are anything we want them to be,
They can be big,
And they can be small,
But what if dreams could make a difference?

Dreams are anything we want them to be,
Dreams of a job,
Dreams of freedom,
Dreams of an education.

Dreams are anything we want them to be,
Dreams of hope,
Dreams of a car,
Dreams of peace.

The world can be anything we want it to be.

Imagine
A clean, safe world

Imagine
A world of peace and freedom

Imagine
A world without poverty

Imagine
If a dream could change the world

Dreams are anything we want them to be,
They can be big,
And they can be small,
And they can make a difference.

Dreams can change the world.

Maybe we should try.

Elizabeth Smith (15)
Thomas Alleynes High School, Uttoxeter

What Are Dreams?

What are dreams?
Sources of terror and calm
Hope and despair
Lands without logic
Foods without taste
Yet we follow them on
In the hope they are true
In the hope they are better
Than that which we know.

But is it the dream
That pushes us on
Or is it the hope
That holds back despair?

But maybe things will get worse left alone
Does hope affect
Our spiral of destruction
Maybe we need to work on our own
To take hold of our fate
And control where we're going

So stop relying on fate,
Stop believing in dreams,
Everything you need,
Is there in the mirror.

James Teasdale (14)
Thomas Alleynes High School, Uttoxeter

I Have A Dream

A is for anger,
B is for bravery,
C is for courage,
D is for dreams,
E is for encourage,
F is for friends,
G is for greatness,
H is for help,
I is for imagine,
J is for jealousy,
K is for knowledge,
L is for love,
M is for majestic,
N is for nervous,
O is for optimistic,
P is for passion,
Q is for quiet,
R is for radiant,
S is for sensible,
T is for tremendous,
U is for united,
V is for venomous,
W is for wonderful,
X is for excellence,
Y is for youthful,
Z is for zest.

Pete Hoptroff (14)
Thomas Alleynes High School, Uttoxeter

I Have A Dream

I have a dream . . .
That the world will all live as equals
I have a dream . . .
That poverty, racism and abuse will be no more,
I have a dream . . .
That the homeless will have homes,
And the abused will live in safety,
I have a dream . . .
That war will stop
And the world will live as one
I believe . . .
That we can live as equals
I believe . . .
That only we can stop people's torture
I believe . . .
That we can help the homeless,
And abused live their lives in joy
I believe . . .
That we will live as one!

Phil Browning (13)
Thomas Alleynes High School, Uttoxeter

Imagine

I have a dream
The world will live in peace
I have a dream
The world will come together
I have a dream
The world will unite
I have a dream
Wars will stop, walls will fall
The countries will stand together.

I imagine,
A world of peace,
I imagine,
A world that is together,
I imagine,
A united world,
I imagine,
No wars, no walls
Countries that stand together.

I see this place,
We can reach it,
If we just stand together.

Matt James (14)
Thomas Alleynes High School, Uttoxeter

I Have A Dream

All of us have dreams,
Maybe some more than others,
Like no homework,
No brothers,
Or something special,
Like get well soon to sick mothers.

But nevertheless we all have them,
All running through our minds,
But what happened to important ones,
From past important times,
Such as the dreams of Martin Luther King,
Of union and fairness,
Was it true then
Is it true now?
Or just the perfect daydream we all have?

Katy O'Brien (14)
Thomas Alleynes High School, Uttoxeter

Hope

If only there was hope,
In the world we are in,
Because it's needed everywhere,
For our soldiers in Iraq,
It's needed most,
So just hope,
Do not despair.

For they brought hope,
To the Iraqi people,
And for that,
They deserve it back,
For they would sacrifice themselves,
For a better place,
For a better Iraq.

Elliot Allison (14)
Thomas Alleynes High School, Uttoxeter

I Believe

I believe
Life is for a reason
I believe
It should be treasured
I believe
Everyone is equal
I believe
You should be individual

I believe
Everyone is entitled to the same things
I believe
Poverty should not be in this world
I believe
War should not exist
I believe
Everyone is equal, but no one the same.

Paul Slaney (13)
Thomas Alleynes High School, Uttoxeter

What Is A Dream?

What is a dream? A dream is a belief.

One person's dream
Is another's nightmare
What is a dream?
Only a dreamer knows
Dreams can come true
Dreams can upset
What is a dream?
A thought in the head
Dreams can last
Dreams can be forgotten
What is a dream?
Do they speak the truth?
Dreams can . . .
Dreams can . . .

Jacques Coetzee (14)
Thomas Alleynes High School, Uttoxeter

I Have A Dream

If only our world had no greed,
No starvation, no poverty, no want
If only our world had no war,
No killing, no murder, no conflict
If only our world had no disease,
No pain, no suffering, no desperation
If only our world had no discrimination,
No racism, no prejudice, no inequality

If only our world had no selfishness,
No thoughtlessness, no inconsiderateness, no unkindness
If only our world had no bullying,
No ridicule, no mockery, no harassment
If only our world had no deceit,
No lying, no blackmail, no falseness
If only our world had no undervalue,
No presuming, no take for granted, no ungratefulness

If only our world had more respect,
More esteem, more admiration, more value
If only our world had more individuality,
More personality, more courage, more bravery
If only our world had more willing to help,
More need to succeed, more consideration, more sharing
If only our world had more love,
More initiative, more unity, more peace.

If only . . .

Sarah Flavell (14)
Thomas Alleynes High School, Uttoxeter

I Have A Dream Poem

A is for aggression to be abolished,
B is for blame to be banished,
C is for cancer to be cured,
D is for death to be dissolved,
E is for execution to be executed,
F is for fear to be fought,
G is for grief to be grasped,
H is for hunger to be harnessed,
I is for infidelity to be eradicated,
J Is for jealousy to be joked,
K is for killing to be killed,
L is for lying to be lost,
M is for murders to be mashed,
N is for nightmares to be nursed,
O is for oppression to be opposed,
P is for problems to be pacified,
Q is for qualms to be quit,
R is for racism to be racked,
S is for sexism to be slain,
T is for torture to be tamed,
U is for unease to be unmasked,
V is for vandalism to be vanquished,
W is for war to be . . . what?
X is for extortion to be extinct
Y is for yelling to be yawned at
Z is for zero hour to be zapped.

Jake Thomas (14)
Thomas Alleynes High School, Uttoxeter

Fairy Tales

Once upon a time,
People were happy and life was fine,
People helped each other,
People lived as a family, father and mother.

Now, time has changed and so have perceptions,
People controlled by money,
People obsessed by hate,
People judged on their skin.

In the future,
Time will change,
So, hopefully, will perceptions,
People will be happy and life will be great,
People will be controlled by their own fate,
People will enjoy each other,
People will care for one another,
No matter what the colour of their skin,
People will treat them as their kin,
Let us not fail,
To make our future real,
And not but another fairy tale.

Matthew McNeice (13)
Thomas Alleynes High School, Uttoxeter

I Dream . . .

One voice in the darkness,
Echoes through the night,
Engulfed by the darkness,
Until there is one light.

One light in the darkness,
Shining through and through,
Joined by one more,
And then there are two.

Two people for one cause,
Still unheard in the world,
No one wants to hear them,
Until someone gets hurt.

Everybody hears them,
And wants justice to be done,
People from different countries,
Want to all be joined as one.

Fighting for the justice,
Fighting for what's right,
Fighting against racism,
I dream we win this fight.

Demi Wibberley (14)
Thomas Alleynes High School, Uttoxeter

Difference?

Chav, Emo, Rockers and Punks
What is in the different looks?
Make-up, clothes, jewellery and hair,
They differ between us, but who cares?

Name-calling, bullying and prejudice
Labelling causes all of this,
The fashion it changes and you choose it,
But the distress it causes is not a benefit.

Why can't we live in the same place?
Does it matter if we wear make-up on our face?
Does it matter if we dress differently?
Why can't girls dress defiantly?

So what if we did live in harmony,
What if it was flowers, hearts and ponies?
Would our dreams, ambitions and plans take place?
What would the world be like with just one race?

There would be no fights in this street,
If we could live together in peace and turn the heat,
This would be fabulous but could it happen,
This is my dream of a world with more passion!

Alice Lewis (14)
Thomas Alleynes High School, Uttoxeter

With My Hair Across My Face

I don't ask for much,
My life is sad. My life is a disgrace,
But my life is also amazing, fantastic
Maybe even perfect
I make my life. Not you. Not him or her.
I do the best I can to sculpt and shape it
So that I can fit into it comfortably
People tell me to add a piece or chip a bit off all the time
But I can't,
Because it won't fit,
My life isn't for you. It's for me.
My size, my measurements. You'll never be contained in it.
You'll shrink to the bottom of it.
Or break through its crust.
Even if you're just like me - in almost every way.
You'd never be comfortable in me.
So if you see me,
Walking past you in the rain or in the wind,
With my hair across my face,
And my bloodshot eyes glaring at the floor,
Look at me. Judge me. Go ahead. I don't mind.
But don't try to copy.
And don't try to change me.

Lucas Shaw (15)
Thomas Alleynes High School, Uttoxeter

Think About It

Think about it
A place where people of all cultures stand as one,
A place where fights are unheard of and people party,
A place of tranquillity with schools full of children of all cultures
A place where racism is dead.

Think about it,
People of black and white living together as one,
People not judging others based purely on their appearance,
People believing in themselves and living a life worth living,
People living in harmony - against all odds.

Think about it,
Racism - a thing of the past
Racism - so cruel and unnecessary
Racism - for people of cowardice with bottled up anger
Racism - a non existent word

Think about it,
Pain, suffering, anguish, hatred, despair,
Death,
Or,
Freedom, united, together, happiness, peace,
One!

You think about it,
You imagine,
You choose!

Charlotte Machin (14)
Thomas Alleynes High School, Uttoxeter

A Turned Back And A Cold Heart

I dream of the day,
She never walks away,
Leaving me with nothing more,
Than her scent and smile,
I dream of the day,
I can enfold her life,
Her life in mine . . .

Her back is turned,
She's walked away for today,
I carry on all alone,
Lying in my bed,
Staring at the ceiling,
I feel so useless,
All I can do is stare . . .

I can't lay here and stare,
My mind wonders pointlessly,
I need to know that she's safe,
I want to hear her voice,
Echoing in my soul . . .

My dream seems so far away,
Oppressed by the ones,
Trying to hide her from me,
I won't give in,
This you will see,
I dream endlessly,
Of the day I can enfold her life in mine,
You will never crush my dream,
To crush my dream is to crush her,
This you will not do,
This you cannot do because she is everything to me . . .

Andrew Smy (14)
Thomas Alleynes High School, Uttoxeter